0 Fin

ne, C.
mind of its own.

RICE: $30.79 (3582/02   )

A Mind of Its Own

*How your brain distorts
and deceives*

Cordelia Fine

Published in the UK in 2006
by Icon Books Ltd., The Old Dairy,
Brook Road, Thriplow, Cambridge SG8 7RG
email: info@iconbooks.co.uk
www.iconbooks.co.uk

Published in Australia in 2005
by Allen & Unwin Pty. Ltd.,
PO Box 8500, 83 Alexander Street,
Crows Nest, NSW 2065

Sold in the UK, Europe, South Africa
and Asia by Faber and Faber Ltd.,
3 Queen Square, London WC1N 3AU
or their agents

Distributed in the UK, Europe, South Africa
and Asia by TBS Ltd., Frating Distribution Centre,
Colchester Road, Frating Green, Colchester CO7 7DW

ISBN 1 84046 678 2

Text copyright © 2005 Cordelia Fine

Typesetting by Wayzgoose

Printed and bound in the UK
by Mackays of Chatham plc

For Russell

Cordelia Fine studied Experimental Psychology at Oxford University, followed by an M.Phil in Criminology at Cambridge University and a Ph.D in Psychology at University College London. She is currently a Research Fellow at the Centre for Applied Philosophy and Public Ethics at the University of Melbourne.

Contents

Introduction

Do you feel that you can trust your own brain? So maybe it falters for a moment, faced with the thirteen times table. It may occasionally send you into a room in search of something, only to abandon you entirely. And, if yours is anything like mine, it may stubbornly refuse to master the parallel park. Yet these are petty and ungrateful gripes when we consider all that our brains actually do for us. Never before have we been made so aware of the extraordinary complexity and sophistication of those one hundred billion brain cells that make up the engine of the mind. And barely a day goes by when these gathered neurons aren't exalted in a newspaper article highlighting a newly discovered wonder of their teamwork.

From day to day, we take our brains somewhat for granted, but (particularly with this book in hand) it's likely that you're feeling a little quiet pride on behalf of your own. And, reading books on the subject of its own self aside, what else can't the thing do? After all, it tells you who you are, and what to think, and what's out there in the world around you. Its ruminations, sensations and conclusions are confided to you and you alone. For absolutely everything you know about anything, it is the part of yourself you have to thank. You might think that, if there's one thing in this world you can trust, it's your own brain. You are, after all, as intimate as it is possible to be.

But the truth of the matter – as revealed by the quite extraordinary and fascinating research described in this book – is that your unscrupulous brain is entirely undeserving of your confidence. It has some shifty habits that leave the truth distorted and disguised. Your brain is vainglorious. It deludes you. It is emotional, pigheaded and secretive. Oh, and it's also a bigot. This is more than a minor inconvenience. That fleshy walnut inside your skull is all you have in order to know yourself and to know the world. Yet, thanks to the masquerading of an untrustworthy brain with a mind of its own, much of what you think you know is not quite as it seems.

The Vain Brain

For a softer, kinder reality

A week after Icon commissioned this book, I discovered that I was pregnant with my second child. The manuscript was due three days before the baby. My husband, a project manager both by temperament and employ, drew up a project plan for me. To my eye, it entirely failed to reflect the complexity, subtlety, and unpredictability of the process of writing a book. It was little more than a chart showing the number of words I had to write per week, and when I was going to write them. It also had me scheduled to work every weekend until the baby was born.

'This plan has me scheduled to work every weekend until the baby is born', I said.

'Plus all the annual leave from your job', my husband added.

I felt that he had missed the point. 'But when do I *rest*?'

'Rest?' My husband pretended to examine the plan. 'As I see it, you rest for two days after you finish the manuscript, shortly before going into labour, giving birth, and becoming the sole source of nutrition for a newborn.'

I had a brief image of myself in labour, telling the midwife between gasps of gas what a treat it was to have some time to myself.

'What if I can't do it?' I asked.

My husband gave me a 'this really isn't difficult' look. '*This* is how you do it', he said, stabbing the plan. 'You write this many words a week.'

He was right, I told myself. Of course I could do it. It was irrelevant that I was pregnant. After all, growing a baby is easy – no project plan required. My first trimester nausea and exhaustion would soon pass. The brains of other, weaker women might be taken hostage by pregnancy hormones, but not my brain. My bump would remain well enough contained to enable me to reach the computer keyboard. And absolutely, definitely, without a doubt, the baby would not come inconveniently early. Of course I could write the book.

I then did something very foolish. I began research on this chapter – the vain brain. The vain brain that embellishes, enhances and aggrandises you. The vain brain that excuses your faults and failures, or simply rewrites them out of history. The vain brain that sets you up on a pedestal above your peers. The vain brain that misguidedly thinks you invincible, invulnerable and omnipotent. The brain so *very* vain that it even considers the letters that appear in your name to be more attractive than those that don't.[1]

I didn't want to know any of this. But then it got worse. I went on to read just how essential these positive illusions are. They keep your head high and your heart out of your boots. They keep you from standing atop railway bridges gazing contemplatively at approaching trains. Without a little deluded optimism, your immune system begins to wonder whether it's worth the effort keeping you alive. And most extraordinary, it seems that sometimes your vain brain manages to transform its grandiose beliefs into reality. Buoyed by a brain that loves you like a mother, you struggle and persevere – happily blind to your own inadequacies, arrogantly dismissive of likely obstacles – and actually achieve your goals.

I needed my vain brain back. *Immediately.*

As evidenced by the existence of this book, I managed to regain my positive illusions. (Either that or I truly *am* exceptional, talented, and blessed by the gods.) Now it's time for me to attempt to spoil your chances of happiness, health and success by disillusioning you.

While it troubles philosophers, for the rest of us it is vastly more comfortable that we can only know ourselves and the world through the distorting lens of our brains. Freud suggested that the ego 'rejects the unbearable idea', and since then experimental psychologists have been peeling back the protective layers encasing your self-esteem to reveal the multitude of strategies your brain uses to keep your ego plump and self-satisfied. Let's start with some basic facts. When asked, people will modestly, reluctantly confess that they are, for example, more ethical, more nobly motivated employees, and better drivers than the average person.[2] In the latter case, this even includes people interviewed in hospital shortly after extraction from the mangled wrecks that were once their cars. No one considers themselves to fall in the bottom half of the heap, and statistically, that's not possible. But in a sample of vain brains, it's inevitable.

For one thing, if possible your brain will interpret the question in the way that suits you best. If I were asked how my driving compares with others, I would rate myself better than average without hesitation. My driving record at speeds above one mile per hour is flawless. Yet below this speed my paintwork, and any stationary object I am attempting to park near, are in constant peril. These expensive unions between the stationary and the near-stationary are so frequent that at one point I actually considered enveloping the vulnerable portions of my car in bubble-wrap. My mother, in contrast, can reverse with exquisite precision into a parking spot at whiplash speeds. On the other hand, she regularly rams into the back of cars that 'should have gone' at roundabouts. She, too, considers her driving to be superb. You begin to see how everyone is able to stake their claim to the superior half of the driving population. If the trait or skill you're being asked about is helpfully ambiguous, you interpret the question to suit your own idiosyncratic strengths.[3]

Even if you are unambiguously hopeless in an area of life, your brain gets round this by simply diminishing the importance of that skill. I, for example, cannot draw. I am the artistic equivalent of being tone deaf. However this doesn't bother me in the slightest because to my brain, drawing is an unnecessary extra. I can see that it would be useful if one were an artist, but in the same way that it's useful for a contortionist to be able to wrap his legs behind his head. Essential for a small minority, but nothing more than a showy party trick for everyone else.[4] And in a final clever enhancement of this self-enhancement, people believe that their weaknesses are so common that they should hardly even be considered weaknesses, yet their strengths are rare and special.[5]

What these strategies reveal is that a bit of ambiguity can be taken a very long way by a vain brain. The next technique in your brain's arsenal of ego defence exploits ambiguity to the full. When we explain to ourselves and others why things have gone well or badly, we prefer explanations that cast us in the best possible light. Thus we are quick to assume that our successes are due to our own sterling qualities, while responsibility for failures can often be conveniently laid at the door of bad luck or damn fool others. This self-serving bias, as it is known, is all too easy to demonstrate in the psychology lab.[6] People arbitrarily told that they did well on a task (for example, puzzle solving) will take the credit for it, whereas people arbitrarily told that they did badly will assign responsibility elsewhere, such as with their partner on the task. The brain is especially self-advancing when your performance on the task could potentially deliver a substantial bruise to your ego.[7] So people told that puzzle solving is related to intelligence are much more likely to be self-serving than those told that puzzle solving is just something that people who don't like reading books do on trains. The bigger the potential threat, the more self-protective the vain brain becomes. In a final irony, people think that others are more susceptible to the self-serving bias than they are themselves.[8] (Allow yourself a moment to take that sentence fully on board, should you need to.)

Thus when life or psychology researchers are kind enough to leave the reasons for success or failure ambiguous, the self-serving bias is readily and easily engaged to protect and nurture the ego. However, our vain brains aren't completely impervious to reality. No matter how partial my explanation of why I added up the restaurant bill incorrectly, I have no intention of applying for any professorships in mathematics. In a way, this is definitely good. When we lose all sight of our ugly face in reality's mirror, this generally means that we have also lost grip on our sanity. But on the other hand, who wants an ugly face right in their face? We've already seen how the vain brain casts our features at their most flattering angle. We'll now begin to rummage deeper into the brain's bag of tricks. By calling on powerful biases in memory and reasoning, the brain can selectively edit and censor the truth, about both ourselves and the world, making for a softer, kinder, and altogether more palatable reality.

Failure is perhaps the greatest enemy of the ego, and that's why the vain brain does its best to barricade the door against this unwelcome guest. The self-serving bias we've already encountered provides a few extra services to this end. One approach is to tell yourself that, in retrospect, the odds were stacked against you and failure was all but inevitable.

Researchers have found that optimists in particular use this strategy, which has been dubbed 'retroactive pessimism', and it makes failure easier to digest.[9]

'Self-handicappers', as they are called, exploit the self-serving bias in a different way. In self-handicapping, the brain makes sure that it has a non-threatening excuse for failure, should it occur. If you can blame your poor performance in an intelligence test on your lack of effort, for example, then your flattering self-image of your intelligence and competence can remain unchallenged. Self-handicapping also enhances the sweetness of success when it occurs, creating a win-win situation for your ego. Drug use, medical symptoms, anxiety, depression ... they can all be used to shield the ego from failure. Take, for example, a group of students who reported suffering severe anxiety during tests. According to a trio of refreshingly brusque researchers, the brains of these devious strategists exploit their test anxiety, whenever they can, to serve ignoble ends.[10] The researchers gave their test-anxious students a difficult two-part test, purportedly a measure of general intelligence. In the interval between the two parts of the test, the students were asked to say how anxious they were feeling about the test, and how much effort they were putting into it. However, right before this survey, *some* of the students had their potential handicap snatched away from them. They were told that a remarkable feature of the test they were taking was that their score was impervious to anxiety and – no matter how nervous they were – their score would be an accurate measure of their intellectual ability.

This was cunning as well as mean. If test-anxious students merely report how anxious they are feeling, with no self-serving motivations, they should report the same level of anxiety regardless of whether they think that anxiety might reduce their score on the test. However, if the test-anxious students use their anxiety as self-protection against possible failure, then students told that anxiety has no bearing on their test scores should report less anxiety, since it won't serve its usual self-handicapping purpose. This is just what the researchers found. And as if this weren't damning enough, the researchers also exposed a sneaky substitute self-handicapping strategy in the students who weren't able to claim that they'd been hampered by their nerves. In place of their handicap of choice, these students instead claimed to have made less effort on the test. It takes more than a few psychologists to stymie the cunning of a determinedly vain brain.

Even when your brain does accept responsibility when things go wrong, research shows that just a few days later your brain may have conveniently cast off the more unflattering explanations for failure. In one experiment investigating this phenomenon, male university students were given a task that supposedly assessed their 'manual dexterity and cognitive perception coordination'.[11] ('I'm handy and I'm co-ordinated.') You can of course imagine a male ego immediately wanting a piece of that pie. The students were randomly told either that they were dexterous virtuosos of cognitive perception or that, frankly, the average china shop proprietor would more warmly welcome a bull into their shop. The men were then asked to explain why they had done well or badly on the test, either immediately afterwards or a few days later. The students whose vain brains were given a few days to edit the memory of the experiment were much more self-enhancing in their explanations of why they had succeeded or failed, in comparison with the students who were asked for their explanations straight away.

Memory is one of your ego's greatest allies, of course. Good things about ourselves tend to secure a firm foothold in the brain cells, while bad stuff – oopsie – has a habit of losing grasp and slipping away. Imagine being given a personality test, and then a list of behaviours that – according to the test – you are likely to perform. Would you later remember more negative behaviours (such as 'You would make fun of others because of their looks' and 'You would often lie to your parents') or more positive behaviours (such as 'You would help a handicapped neighbour paint his house' or 'You would keep secrets if asked to')? Intuitively you might think that the rather surprising predictions that you are likely to be unkind and untrustworthy would so jar with your generally positive self-concept that they would be more memorable. However, when researchers gave people a bogus personality test of this sort, this is not what they found.[12] Instead, it was the predictions of caring and honourable behaviours that stuck in people's memories. The reason was that their brains simply refused to allocate as much processing time to nasty predictions as to the nice ones. It seems that it is easier for a camel to pass through

the eye of a needle than for negative feedb̶̶̶ ̶̶
enter the kingdom of memory.

Not only does memory collude with the brain in
the information that it lets in but, as you might
begin to fear, it also controls the information it lets
out. All brains contain an enormous database of personal memories that bear on that perennially fascinating question 'Who *am* I?', or the self-concept. But
the self-concept, psychologists have discovered, is
conveniently shifting.[13] If the self-concept you are
wearing no longer suits your motives, the brain
simply slips into something more comfortable. The
willing assistant in this process is memory. It has the
knack of pulling out personal memories that better
fit the new circumstances. Two Princeton researchers
observed this metamorphosis directly, by tempting
the vain brains of their volunteers with an attractive
change of self-concept.[14] They asked a group of
students to read one of two (fabricated) scientific
articles. The first article claimed that an extroverted
personality helps people to achieve academic success.
The second article, handed out to just as many
students, claimed instead that introverts tend to be
more academically successful. You can guess what's

going to happen. Imagine it. You're a vain brain. You're a vain brain at *Princeton*, for goodness' sake. Someone's offering you a shimmering, glittering, dazzling self-concept that says, 'Hey, world. *I* am going to make it.' A personality trait you've been told offers the crystal stairway to triumph might not be quite your size, but if you can make it fit with a bit of tweaking, you will. Whichever personality trait the students thought was the key to success, the more highly the students rated themselves as possessing that attribute.

What happens is that the vain brain calls in memory to make sure that the most attractive self-concept fits. From the enormous wardrobe of rich and complicated autobiographical events from your life, your memory brings to the fore those memories that best match the self-concept you are trying to achieve. When people are told that extroverts, say, tend to be more successful than shy and retiring types, it is the memories that bear out their sociable and outgoing natures that rush quickly and easily to consciousness.[15] And, as we've already seen, memory keeps the gate at the front door as well. Give someone who's been told that one type of personality leads to success a bit of personality feedback, and she will remember much more of the feedback that shows that she possesses the supposedly more favourable attribute.[16]

The vain brain's other powerful protectorate is reasoning. This might seem a little odd. Isn't reasoning supposed to be the compass that guides us towards the truth, not saves us from it? It seems not, particularly when our ego is under attack. In fact, the best we can say of our gift for thinking in these circumstances is that we do at least recognise that conclusions cannot be drawn out of thin air; we need a bit of evidence to support our case. The problem is that we behave like a smart lawyer searching for evidence to bolster his client's case, rather than a jury searching for the truth. As we've seen, memory is often the over-zealous secretary who assists in this process by hiding or destroying files that harbour unwanted information. Only when enough of the objectionable stuff has been shredded dare we take a look. Evidence that supports your case is quickly accepted, and the legal assistants are sent out to find more of the same. However, evidence that threatens reason's most important client – you – is subjected to gruelling cross-examination. Accuracy, validity and plausibility all come under attack in the witness stand. The case is soon won. A victory for justice and truth, you think, conveniently ignoring the fact that yours was the only lawyer in the courtroom.

Time now to watch your hot-shot lawyer in action. Imagine there's a rumour afoot that certain things about you augur badly for how well you will do in your chosen profession. Your reputation is at risk, and your lawyer is engaged to defend you from this potential slander. This was the situation created in a study demonstrating that the client is always right.[17] University students were asked to take part in an experiment about the reasons for success in law, medicine and business. They were given fictitious descriptions of people who supposedly did well or badly at professional school. The sorts of attributes they read about were things like being the youngest or oldest child, being Catholic or Protestant, and having had a mother employed outside the home or a stay-at-home mother.

Now, say one of the students is the youngest child of a Catholic family whose mother stayed at home rearing her and her ten older siblings, and she longs to be a lawyer. Then she reads about a successful lawyer who is Catholic, the oldest child, and whose mother went out to work. Wouldn't it be nice if she could convince herself that the things she has in common with the successful lawyer are what make for success, but that the things they differ on aren't important? This is just what happens. The student decides that a Catholic upbringing brings success, but that the other two factors are relatively unimportant. However, if the student had been told that the same person is *un*successful, suddenly her Catholicism seems far less relevant (what could religion possibly have to do with it?), but birth order and mother's employment – the factors she differs on – suddenly become crucial. Your hard-working lawyer constructs the most flattering and self-serving case it can from the available data.

The next step is the evaluation of evidence. When that evidence poses a threat to your ego, a good lawyer can always find fault. In one such experiment, high-school students were given an intelligence test.[18] Some of them were told that they had done well, others that they had done badly. All of them were also given a few pages to read containing arguments from scientists both for and against the validity of intelligence tests. Even though everyone was given the same information, the poor guinea pigs whose egos had been threatened by negative feedback decided that intelligence tests were a much cruder tool for measuring intellectual depths than did students who were told that they'd done brilliantly. Was this because memory had hidden the pro-intelligence test files? Actually, no. In fact, the ego-threatened students remembered more of the pro-intelligence test arguments than did the others. This seems a little odd, until you consider all the effort the vain brain's lawyer must have put in to disparage those particular arguments. If you spend a great deal of effort crossexamining a witness you'll have a good memory for what they said, even if you don't believe a goddamn word of their lies.

On the whole, people it seems are content to employ the sloppiest of reasoning ... until some threat to our motives appears, at which point we suddenly acquire the strictest possible methodological standards.[19] The smart lawyer inside us is also skilled at finding supporting witnesses to bolster our case. Remember the experiments in which people were told that being either outgoing or withdrawn by nature is more conducive to success? Well, your brain not only biases your memory to make you think that you've been blessed with the more favourable personality attribute. It also then encourages you to spend time in the company of people who think you're really like that.[20]

The lawyer rarely allows you to plead guilty. When you've treated someone in a way you don't feel quite right about, your untiring friend works hard in defence of your character by calling upon mitigating factors. A little sophistry and suddenly it appears that what you did wasn't so bad after all. Or you weren't really responsible. Excuse-making is often studied within the setting of what is called 'bystander apathy'. How was it that none of the 38 witnesses to a fatal stabbing of a young woman in Queens, New York, intervened or called the police? Because 'we thought it was just a lovers' quarrel' or 'I was tired'.[21] In laboratory set-ups, the excuses given by apathetic bystanders are equally remarkable.[22] People who fail to report smoke billowing into a room suggest that it is simply smog or steam. People who don't help a woman who has just fallen off a ladder claim that she hadn't actually fallen, or wasn't really injured. The sleaziest excuse of all is to defend yourself by attacking the victim: he deserved it, she brought it upon herself. In a series of experiments students were asked to watch another student (actually a stooge) receive a large number of painful electric shocks, supposedly as part of a psychology learning experiment. The researchers found that the more uneasy the students felt their role to be in the victim's suffering, the *less* they considered the victim to be a good and likeable person.[23] It's just more comfortable that way.

It's rather unsettling to know that your ego is so very well protected from reality. And it's not just your ego that's kept so safely removed from the truth. Perhaps understandably, given the slings and arrows of fortune we must dodge every day, your vain brain calls upon many of the same strategies to keep your perception of your future health, happiness and fortune pleasantly unrealistic.

Just as we all believe ourselves to be better people than average, so too we think ourselves relatively invulnerable to life's trials. Who, at the wedding altar, is thinking 'Fifty-fifty chance of this working –

let's keep our fingers crossed'? Possibly most of the congregation, but probably not the bride or groom. Remember our Catholic student who made up theories to explain why she was likely to succeed at law school? In the same study the researchers showed that people use the same sort of self-serving speculations to persuade themselves that *their* marriage will be happy.[24] Similarly, people estimate that they will live about ten years longer than actuarial data suggest.[25] I recently came across a website that, on the basis of a few pertinent pieces of information, furnishes you with your likely date of death. (For those with a morbid interest, or the need to make very long-term plans, the website is www.deathclock.com.) From this helpful website I learnt that I would die on Sunday 10 May 2054 at the age of 79. 'That seems very young', I thought, and instantly gave myself another – well – ten years, mostly on the grounds that I have long eschewed sausage meat, a product which must surely substantially impair longevity.

As with anything that threatens our egos, we push our standards for evidence that might challenge our rosy beliefs absurdly high. For example, brains prefer not to have to take too seriously any medical information that challenges our sense of physical invulnerability. My father-in-law enjoys a life-style that, to put it bluntly, would leave the hardiest of cardiologists weeping into their public health information pamphlets. Statistically, he should prob-ably have died shortly before he was born. Con-cerning all those pesky 'smoking – disease – death connection' studies, he is breathtakingly (excuse the pun) dismissive. Yet he is not immune to the charms of scientific discovery when it suits. For example, he never fails to encourage me to push aside my tumb-ler of water in favour of a nice healthy glass of red wine. In an experimental study of this 'motivated scepticism' phenomenon, people were given an article to read that set out the medical dangers for women (but not men) of drinking too much coffee.[26] Men and women who drank little or no coffee found it convincing. Men who drank a lot of coffee found it convincing. There are no prizes for guessing which group thought the link between caffeine and disease unpersuasive.

Vain brains are reluctant to accept hints of phys-ical vulnerability even when it's staring them in the face. In another demonstration of self-protective

incredulity, some volunteers were told about a fictitious medical condition called thioamine acetylase
(TAA) deficiency.[27] TAA-deficient individuals, they
were reliably informed, were 'relatively susceptible to
a variety of pancreatic disorders' later in life. Then
one by one the volunteers were led into a private
room (or was it?) to test themselves for the condition, by dipping a special piece of test paper (or was
it?) into a sample of saliva. Some of the volunteers
were told that if their TAA levels were normal, the
strip would remain yellow. They were the lucky ones.
The rest of the volunteers were told that if their TAA
levels were normal the strip would turn dark green.
They were the unlucky ones. The test strip, being made
of ordinary yellow paper, wasn't going to change
colour no matter how much spit it encountered.

These 'TAA deficiency' volunteers, the ones who
'failed' the saliva reaction test, were determinedly
optimistic about the perils of TAA deficiency. They
reckoned that both TAA deficiency and pancreatic
disease were far less serious and far more common
than did people who 'passed' the test. The 'TAA deficiency' volunteers also rated the saliva reaction test
as less accurate. Even more defensive was their

behaviour while they were taking the saliva test. The researchers were secretly spying on them, of course, while they took the test. Everyone had been told that colour development took from 10 to 60 seconds, but was generally complete within 20. Volunteers were asked to pop their strips into an envelope as soon as the test was done. The 'TAA deficiency' volunteers were much slower to do this, giving their yellow paper a generous extra half a minute or so to change colour, compared with the 'no deficiency' volunteers. What's more, the majority of the 'deficiency' volunteers engaged in some kind of illicit re-testing to help their recalcitrant strips along. Some people used a fresh saliva sample. Others re-tested using a new strip. Some placed the strip directly onto their tongue. The strips were shaken, blown, wiped, and saturated with enormous volumes of saliva. These volunteers didn't like their diagnosis and they were seeking second, third and fourth opinions on the matter.

Vain brains can even trick us into unconsciously manipulating the outcome of a medical diagnosis to make it more acceptable. To show this, a group of experimentees were asked to immerse their forearm in a vat of icy cold water (yes, painful) and to keep it there for as long as they could bear.[28] They had to do this both before and after taking physical exercise. Some volunteers were told that if they could keep their arm in the ice-water for longer *after* exercise, that was a sign of long life expectancy. The other volunteers were told the reverse. Although they weren't aware that they were doing so, the volunteers changed their tolerance for the cold water after exercise in whichever direction they'd been told predicted a long and healthy life. Of course, manipulating their tolerance in this way couldn't possibly affect actual life expectancy, but that's not really what's important to a vain brain.

As we draw towards the end of this chapter, there are two morals to be drawn. One, never trust a social psychologist. Two, never trust your brain. They both manipulate your perception of reality, thus tricking you into embarrassing vanities. (Of course, in the case of the social psychologist those vanities are then permanently recorded in order that other professionals may be entertained by them. So perhaps you should trust social psychologists even less than you do your brain.) But don't feel angry with your vain brain for shielding you from the truth. There is in fact a category of people who get unusually close to the truth about themselves and the world. Their self-perceptions are more balanced, they assign responsibility for success and failure more even-handedly, and their predictions for the future are more realistic. These people are living testimony to the dangers of self-knowledge. They are the clinically depressed.[29]

Psychologist Martin Seligman and colleagues have identified a pessimistic 'explanatory style' that is common in depressed people.[30] When pessimists fail they blame themselves, and think that the fault is in themselves ('I'm stupid', 'I'm useless'), will last for ever, and will affect everything they do. This is a far cry from the sorts of explanations that happy, self-serving people give for failure. And it seems that this pessimism can seriously endanger your health. Pessimists make more doctor visits, have weaker immune systems, are less likely to survive cancer, are more likely to suffer recurrent heart disease, and are more likely to meet with untimely death.[31] It may be hard to cultivate a more optimistic perspective in the face of such data, but it's worth trying.

One final glorious reason to thank your vain brain is that the joyous cry of the optimist – 'Sure! I can do that!' – accompanies a strong motivation to persist on difficult tasks.[32] Including perhaps the difficult task of life itself, according to the sensationally named 'Terror Management Theory', developed by a psychologist rejoicing in the surname Pyszczynski.[33] A healthily vain brain is 'a protective shield designed to control the potential for terror that results from awareness of the horrifying possibility that we humans are merely transient animals groping to survive in a meaningless universe, destined only to die and decay'. I'm sure you will agree that if a few positive illusions can keep at bay the disturbing thought that in truth you are of no more significance in the universe than, as Pyszczynski cruelly puts it, 'any individual potato, pineapple, or porcupine', then we all owe a large debt of gratitude to our vain brains.

But let's end on a more comforting note. Although in the grand scheme of things you may not be of more significance than a porcupine, you are almost certainly a better driver.

The Emotional Brain

Sweaty fingers in all the pies

My son, thirteen months old, is crying as if his heart will break. He sobs with his entire body, and I know that in a few seconds he will assume what my husband and I call 'The Tragedy Pose'. Sure enough, soon he collapses onto the floor and flops forward so that his forehead hits the carpet. I am holding in my hand the accomplice to the act that has obliterated all joy from my son's existence. This object and I, between us, have left no other course available to my young child but to give himself over completely to unmitigated, carpet-drenching grief. I struggle painfully but successfully with the urge to ruin his character for ever by returning to him this item upon which, clearly, his entire happiness depends. It is a ballpoint pen.

As it happens, I know just how it feels to have

ballpoint pens taken away. My husband, as part of his Stationery Stationing System, has strategically located pens at three key note-making points around the house: clipped onto the calendar; by the phone; and in the travel wallet. According to the System, these pens should only ever be removed from their posts to be used for, respectively, noting events on the calendar, taking down phone messages, and filling in travel-related documents. My husband is quite strict in his enforcement of this rule, and any pen found being used for a purpose other than that intended is immediately returned to its sentry-post.

And irritating though it is to have a writing implement removed mid-word, I simply do not seem to feel the loss as keenly as does my son. For this I have my prefrontal cortex to thank. A mere smudge of brain cells at birth, it takes twenty-odd years or more to reach its full stature as the sergeant major of the adult brain. One of the many jobs of the prefrontal cortex is to regulate the emotional responses of less civilised brain regions, which is why it's such a useful thing to have. While doing my PhD, I studied a man who had damaged part of his prefrontal cortex in a car accident. Because he had a little problem with his temper (he liked to let an iron bar do his arguing for him), for the safety of all he had been removed to a high security psychiatric hospital. I made the mistake of reading his case notes just before meeting him and I felt deeply nervous as to how the two of us would hit it off. Unfortunately, when I am anxious my palms become unpleasantly sweaty. As I began to shake hands with the patient, he rapidly withdrew his own with an expression of the utmost disgust, and ostentatiously wiped it on his trousers.

'Christ!' he remarked to my supervisor, who was relishing every moment. 'It's like shaking hands with a wet haddock.'

Had his prefrontal cortex been intact and doing its job, I have no doubt that he would have kept this observation to himself.

There is little doubt that, compared with the toddler or the uninhibited brain-damaged patient, we display a truly authoritative control of our emotions. Nonetheless, it is also the case that our emotions enjoy an impressive mastery of us. It may seem, as we busily go about our lives making decisions and passing judgment on people and events, that we are making good use of our uniquely human powers of rationality. However, research suggests that it is often our emotions that are actually wearing the pants.

Psychologists have become fascinated in recent years by the clout our emotions wield over our decisions. The experiment that sparked off this interest used a gambling game as a laboratory simulation of the complex and uncertain mix of risks and benefits that our everyday choices bring. The researchers asked volunteers to select cards, over and over, from any of the four decks in front of them.[34] They weren't given much information about the decks, just that some worked out better than others. When they turned over a card they learnt whether they had won or lost points. Two of the decks yielded high point gains but, every so often, very severe point losses. This meant that, overall, these packs were best avoided. The other two packs were actually more beneficial in the long run; they offered less dazzling point wins, but less devastating point losses. While the volunteers played the game, the researchers monitored their emotional responses. They did this by measuring their 'skin conductance response' – the polite way of referring to how much someone is sweating. (Skin conductance equipment measures the electrical conductivity of skin, which is affected by the salt in sweat.)

The pattern of winning and losing was too complicated for the volunteers to calculate which decks were the best. Yet by the end of the experiment, nearly all of the volunteers were choosing from the winning packs. They had developed 'hunches' about which decks to avoid. This isn't particularly remarkable in itself, but what was rather eerie was that the volunteers' sweaty fingers seemed to work out which decks to avoid before the volunteers themselves did. In the 'pre-hunch' stage, while the volunteers were still choosing cards haphazardly, their skin conductance responses would shoot up just before they chose a card from a losing deck. Only *after* the volunteers started showing these warning emotional jolts did they develop their gut feeling that they should avoid those decks.

The authority that these gut feelings have over our behaviour became clear when the researchers gave the same gambling game to a patient with damage to part of the prefrontal cortex (the ventromedial prefrontal lobe). This man, known as EVR, had been a happy and successful businessman, husband and father until a brain tumour developed in part of his prefrontal cortex and had to be removed. Soon after, EVR's professional and personal life went to rack and ruin because of an extraordinary inability to make decisions. The simplest purchases – which razor to buy? what brand of shampoo? – required exhaustive comparisons of price and quality. And you could faint from hunger waiting for him to decide at which restaurant to eat. He would begin with an extensive discussion of each restaurant's seating plan, details of its menu, its atmosphere, and its management. Then the field work would begin, in the form of drive-by inspections to see how busy each restaurant was. Yet even after all this research, EVR still found it impossible to choose.[35] EVR's pathological vacillation was so time-consuming that it placed a terminal strain on both his marriage and his employment. And when he did manage to make decisions, they were generally bad ones. Despite numerous warnings from others that he was making a terrible mistake, this once shrewd businessman invested all his savings in a home-building business with a partner of dubious commercial and moral credentials, and went bankrupt.

What was so odd about EVR's condition – and what made it so hard to understand why his post-surgery life was so disastrous – was that his intellect was completely unaffected by his brain injury. The researchers studying him chatted with him for hours about current affairs, politics and ethics, and were unfailingly impressed with his intelligence and knowledge. They quizzed him too on hypothetical social dilemmas, asking him what a person could and should do in tricky social situations. EVR had no trouble in coming up with a whole range of sensible solutions to these problems even though – as he himself cheerfully admitted – he wouldn't have a clue what to decide to do if he ended up in those situations himself.[36]

In fact, it was partly this strange unconcern about his problems that triggered the researchers' suspicions that EVR's failing might be an emotional one. Nothing seemed to touch him emotionally, and this was confirmed by an experiment showing that EVR (and other patients like him) didn't show normal skin conductance increases to emotionally charged pictures (such as scenes of mayhem, mutilation and nudity).[37] Could it be that this emotional lack was behind EVR's debilitating incapacity to make decisions? The researchers investigated this idea using their gambling game, monitoring the skin conductance responses of EVR and other similar patients while they played. In the game, as in life, the patients made poor decisions, never learning to avoid the 'bad' decks. This was despite the fact that half of the patients even came to realise that the high-risk decks they were going for were bad news.[38]

Why couldn't the patients 'solve' the gambling task? Unlike the non-brain-damaged volunteers – who let off an emotional skin conductance 'shudder' right before choosing from a bad deck, even before they consciously began to suspect that those decks should be avoided – the patients showed no signs of building up this sort of 'emotional knowledge'. The conclusion it is most tempting to draw is that these emotional 'tags' (or 'somatic markers', as the researchers called them) guide our decision-making. Without these emotional tags, even the most encyclopedic knowledge or powerful intellect cannot help us to pluck a bottle of shampoo off the supermarket shelf.

What is more, it seems that our emotions may be crucially involved in far loftier judgments than selecting toiletries. Even our moral condemnations and approbations usually stem from instant gut feelings or 'moral intuitions',[39] according to one recent hypothesis. As we ponder a morally charged situation we feel a primitive flash of emotion, which is all we need in order to pass our judgment. However – it being a shame to leave resting idle those parts of our brain that help to distinguish us from the apes – we then invent reasons to explain and justify our view. (And, as you will see in 'The Pigheaded Brain', the brain is disturbingly adept at supplying a conveniently biased array of evidence and arguments to bolster our opinions.) This gives us the satisfying, though illusory, impression that our morals are based on reasoned and logical thought rather than cartoon-esque reflexes such as 'yuk!', 'ouch!' or 'tsk!'. Thanks to the emotional brain's clever deception, it normally seems – both to ourselves and to others – that we engaged in our skilful cogitation before, rather than after, forming our moral verdict. Yet when there are no good reasons around to justify our knee-jerk responses, the fact that we are grasping at

non-existent straws of rational thought in the moral-
ising process becomes embarrassingly apparent.

For example, researchers at the University of
Virginia in the United States asked students to justify
their moral condemnation of (I shall put this as
delicately as I am able) a man self-pleasuring with the
willing assistance of a dog.[40] According to the Western
framework of morality which can be summed up
crudely as 'anything goes, so long as nobody gets hurt',
icky though it is to contemplate, there is nothing
morally wrong with this mutually enjoyable interaction between a man and his best friend. That's why
many of the students had a hard time rationalising
their reflexive 'yuk' responses, becoming 'morally
dumbfounded' as the researchers put it. 'Well, I just,
I don't know, I don't think that's, I guess [long
pause], I don't really [laughter] think of these things
much, so I don't really know but, I don't know, I just
[long pause], um …' was one student's inarticulate
attempt to explain her censure of the man-with-dog
scenario, for example. Moral intuitions based on
unthinking emotions may not always serve us too
well, then, if our aim is a coherent and consistent
moral framework. Our own discomfort or disgust

may not always be compatible with the moral principles to which we claim to subscribe.

And there is further peril in using our emotions as information – the danger of mistaking the cause of those emotions. If we misattribute our emotion to the wrong source – thinking it stems from some origin other than the one that is actually causing our surge of feeling – this error can be 'carried forward' to our judgments and decisions. Why do white jurors judge the killers of white victims more harshly than they do the killers of black people? One suggestion is that the murder of a white person triggers a stronger emotional response in the juror, which is 'added in' to the juror's moral calculations about the heinousness of the crime.[41] And research does indeed suggest that emotions may be wrongly introduced into our mental equations surprisingly often.

The problem is that our bodies seem to produce a 'one size fits all' emotional response. For a long time some psychologists had trouble accepting the idea that our hearts thump in pretty much the same way regardless of whether we're in an exam, have just won the lottery, or are running for a bus.[42] These die-hard psychologists went to extraordinarily elaborate lengths in their attempts to show that the body responds differently to different emotions. And they spared no amount of emotional trauma in their volunteers along the way. (This was before the concept of 'research ethics', way back in the golden era of psychology when you could hurl an unsuspecting volunteer into the throes of a powerfully distressing emotion and then all have a laugh about it afterwards.) For example, a researcher with the suitably ominous name of Ax asked volunteers to lie down on a medical bed.[43] He then attached them to a complicated tangle of electrodes and wires, and told them to relax. Once they were nice and comfy, unexpectedly, they began to feel electric shocks in their little finger. When they commented on this to the experimenter, he feigned surprise and twiddled a few knobs. Moments later, sparks began to fly across the wires and the experimenter, lab-coat flying with panic, exclaimed that there was a dangerous high voltage short circuit. The volunteer lay awaiting fatal electrocution for about five minutes while the experimenter flapped about creating 'an atmosphere of alarm and confusion', until he finally declared the short circuit repaired and the danger over.

There was no doubt that Ax's volunteers were genuinely scared. One volunteer remarked afterwards, 'Well, everybody has to go some time. I thought this might be my time.' Another volunteer prayed to God to be spared death. Yet despite the admirable success of Ax and others in inducing gut-wrenching emotions in their volunteers, it was all in vain. They failed to discover any interesting differences between the physiology of the volunteer trembling with terror and wondering whether his will is in order, and the volunteer about to, say, keel over dead from rage. It is the thoughts that go alongside your emotional arousal that enable you to distinguish between one emotion and another. There's no great mystery to human emotions. All you need to know is one simple equation:[44]

EMOTION = AROUSAL + EMOTIONAL THOUGHTS

Because the arousal is the same whatever the emotion – it varies only in intensity – your brain has the job of matching the arousal with the right thoughts. In fact, when it comes to emotions, your brain is a bit like a laundry assistant matching socks in a hurry before his tea break. When you have two socks that are bright blue with a cartoon dog on them, there's no trouble matching them together. (My brain had little difficulty pairing finding myself confined in a small room with a dangerously uninhibited frontal lobe patient with my sweaty palms.) But when it comes to pairing up all those workaday socks that are only slightly different lengths, styles and hues of black, things get a bit trickier. And your brain isn't all that careful. In lieu of a perfect match, it's happy to snatch up any old black sock that looks about right. The consequence of this is that you attribute your arousal to the wrong thing.

In one such experiment, researchers asked three groups of men to ride an exercise bike for long enough to build up a decent sheen of sweat.[45] They were then given the arduous task of watching an erotic film, and reporting their level of sexual arousal. The first group of men watched and rated the film for its sexually invigorating nature long after they'd recovered from the exercise. Their brains didn't have any problems because there were only two socks to match: the arousal from looking at naked women, and thoughts about the naked women. The second group of men viewed the film straight after taking the exercise. Their brains weren't fooled either. They easily matched the extra arousal with the exercise, and the arousal from the naked women with the thoughts about the naked women. But the last group saw the film a little while after the exercise. By this time, although the men were still physically aroused from the cycling, they weren't aware of it. They had, as it were, lost a sock. This meant that they tidily paired up the arousal from the film *and* the arousal from the exercise bike with their thoughts about the film. As a result, they rated themselves as significantly more excited by the film than did the other two groups of men. Their emotional brains misled them about how erotic they had found the film. (You might want to bear this experiment in mind next time someone starts flirting with you at the water cooler in the gym: they may have read this book.)

Our emotional brains also leave our judgments vulnerable to the influence of our moods. When you are walking on the sunny side of the street, your worries really do seem to be left behind on the doorstep. Life seems more satisfying, the grim reaper seems less industrious, politicians even seem less offensive when you are in a cheerful frame of mind.[46] And it can be a remarkably trivial event that tints our spectacles in this rosy fashion. In one classic experiment, a researcher lurking in a shopping mall posed as a company representative and offered some customers (but not others) a small gift, to 'introduce them to the company's products'.[47] Then a second researcher standing a short way away asked them (as part of a 'customer survey') to rate the performance of their cars and televisions. The free gift was about as desirable as the contents of a mid-range Christmas cracker. Nonetheless, it put the customers who received it into a rather jolly mood, compared with the others. These happy customers – clutching their newly acquired nail-clippers – rated their cars and TVs significantly more positively than did the customers without gifts.

Gloom has just the opposite effect on our view of life. Flu symptoms seem more troublesome, relationship conflicts seem more of our own doing, and racial minorities seem less likeable when we are in a bad mood.[48] Psychologists are still squabbling over exactly how and when moods influence our judgments.[49] However, it looks as though at least some of the time our moods mislead us in the same way that misattributed arousal can. If we haven't registered why we're in a particular mood, then sometimes we erroneously use that mood to inform our opinions about things. When researchers rang students on either a sunny or a rainy day, and asked them about their current happiness and their satisfaction with life in general, the students contacted during fine weather were in better moods than the students contacted while it was raining.[50] In line with what we've already learnt, their weather-influenced mood affected the students' satisfaction with their lives: students contacted on sunny days were more satisfied with their lives. However, other students, asked casually at the start of the interview, 'By the way, how's the weather down there?' didn't let their present mood colour or confuse their judgments when it came to their feelings about their life satisfaction. Reminded by the telephone surveyor that their mood was probably due to the weather, these students successfully and appropriately must have dismissed their spirits as irrelevant to the question in hand.

It is surprising enough that, as all this research shows, those squeakings and creakings of the emotional brain in action can wield such a heft of power over our behaviour and judgments, often without our even noticing its influence. Perhaps more surprising still, though, is the role that these very emotions play in generating our sense of self. Indeed, the more we learn, the more even the most thoughtful philosopher or the most determined contemplative would have to admit that it is not thoughts, but the emotions, that make the miracle of our existence real to us. They seem to be what generate our very sense of existence, or *being*.

Think back to the most nerve-wracking experience of your life. Did you feel as if you weren't actually there? It's very likely that you felt an eerie detachment from yourself, as if some sort of 'out-of-body you' were dispassionately observing you. Perhaps most curious of all is that, rather than experiencing the shakes and quakes merited by the situation, you felt peculiarly emotionless.

My own traumatic experience of this sort occurred in the unlikely venue of a science museum. I was newly employed as an 'Explainer', a lone psychologist amid a cluster of biochemists. These über-Explainers pipetted, centrifuged and chromatographed their way through the training with ease, while I knocked over the test tubes of myself and others, and wished that I had been born with hands rather than paws. While the biochemists admired the genetic material they had cleverly unleashed from onion cells – an activity deemed suitable for children aged five and up – I gazed bewildered at my *soupe d'oignon*, and not a chromosome in sight.

By the day of my first workshop my well-founded anxieties about my competence were alleviated only by the knowledge that I would be joined by one of the superbly competent Explainers. I anticipated expertly assisting in the distribution of labcoats and then allowing the biochemist to pull her weight by running the workshop. However, I turned out to be a superior Explainer to her in one important respect. I remembered to attend the workshop.

I was terrified. My mission was to guide twelve pre-pubescents through the Frankensteinian mutation of *E. coli* bacteria. The children were beginning to fidget: some choosing to play with the alarmingly expensive scientific equipment; others preferring to jiggle the flimsy petri dishes containing potentially lethal bacteria. It was at that moment that my brain did a runner. My 'me', so to speak, slipped out of my body and watched impassively as Cordelia Fine ran a science workshop. Thanks to my brain, I was able to do a much better job than if I had remained in there, gripped in the clutch of terror. The *E. coli* may have remained unmutated – and the children possibly wondered what all that scientific equipment was actually *for* – but there were no fatalities or lawsuits. (Despite this, shortly after this incident it was suggested to me that I might prefer to never Explain anything in the museum ever again.)

What I was experiencing in those few hours of intense anxiety was what psychologists call depersonalisation. It's an ace your brain keeps up its sleeve for when the chips are down. You feel detached from your thoughts, feelings and body, and the world may seem dreamy and unreal. Once the coast is clear your brain brings you back again, and the world is real once more.

What is your brain up to during depersonalisation episodes? Thanks to those pesky research ethics that prioritise bothersome issues such as people's welfare and rights over furtherance of scientific knowledge, psychologists can't simply recruit a handful of generous volunteers, throw them into a terrifying situation, and then take a few measurements. Instead, they have been studying people with a psychiatric condition called depersonalisation disorder that leaves them in an almost constant state of out-of-bodyness.[51] Like the depersonalisation you may have experienced yourself, it is often set off by intensely anxious episodes. This is almost certainly no coincidence. Depersonalisation seems to be the emotional brain's emergency response to stress and anxiety. In the face of severe threat, your brain throws up its hands in defeat and switches off the emotions at the mains. This prevents you from becoming overwhelmed with anxiety, which could be literally fatal in a dangerous situation.

But if the emotions are off, they're off. There aren't separate stopcocks for 'crazy psychologist telling me I'm about to be electrocuted to death' emotions and 'damn, I've got a parking ticket' emotions. So if the theory about depersonalisation is right, patients should be unemotional about everything. Sure enough, when psychologists showed depersonalisation disorder patients nasty pictures, they didn't show the normal leap in skin conductance response.[52] The patients just weren't emotionally aroused by the unpleasant pictures in the way people usually are.

The same researchers then looked directly into the brains of the depersonalisation patients using functional magnetic resonance imaging, the whizz-bang imaging technology that measures brain activity.[53] They wanted to see how the patients' brains responded to disgusting things. Going round to the patients' houses and performing an enema on the kitchen table wasn't on the cards (darn those research ethics committees) so it was back to the pictures. Normally, a part of the brain called the insula goes wild when you see disgusting things. It's the part of your brain that stays forever eight years old. But the insulas of the depersonalisation patients actually responded *less* to disgusting pictures than they did to boring pictures. What *was* getting overly excited, however, was our old friend the prefrontal cortex.

Because the prefrontal cortex is in charge of keeping our emotions in check, there is a huge amount of communication between the prefrontal cortex and areas of the brain like the insula that respond to emotional stimuli. This is why it was so interesting that the sergeant major of the brain was over-active in the patients with depersonalisation disorder when they looked at disgusting pictures in the brain imaging study. Unlike my charming patient with the damaged prefrontal cortex, whose emotions were allowed to run wild and free, the prefrontal cortices of the depersonalisation disorder patients seemed to be holding the emotions on too tight a rein. It looked as if, at the merest glimpse of something a little juicy, the prefrontal cortex started shooting commands down to the insula, warning it to keep its mouth shut. This excessive nannying by your prefrontal cortex may be how your emotional brain is able to shut itself off during depersonalisation episodes.

It might seem rather appealing, the idea of remaining so untouched by the emotional flotsam of life. One imagines depersonalisation patients greeting an astronomical phone bill with a lackadaisical shrug, a leaking roof with a careless laugh. But in fact depersonalisation is an extremely unpleasant state to be in for any length of time. Self-injury and self-mutilation aren't uncommon in depersonalisation patients, perhaps as an attempt to just feel *something*. Life is flat and disturbingly unreal:[54]

Music usually moves me, but now it might as well be someone mincing potatoes … I seem to be walking about in a world I recognise but don't feel … It's the terrible isolation from the rest of the world that frightens me. It's having no contact with people or my husband. I talk to them and see them, but I don't feel they are really here.

As one patient put it, 'I would rather be dead than continue living like this. It is like the living dead.' That's the problem with depersonalisation. You no longer feel as if you're experiencing life:

It is as if the real me is taken out and put on a shelf or stored somewhere inside of me. Whatever makes me me is not there.

I feel as though I'm not alive – as though my body is an empty, lifeless shell.

This is what suggests that it is our emotional brain that gifts us with our sense of self. It is our emotions, no matter how trivial, that let us know we are alive.[55] We see the toilet seat left up *again*, and the brain chuckles, 'Yep, still here.' If this is true then, in theory, if the emotions were shut off tight enough a person might actually begin to believe that they no longer exist ...

> One day I went out for a walk, right round town and ended up at my mother-in-law's and said to her, 'I'm dead' and started stabbing at my arm to try and get some blood out. It wouldn't bleed so I was saying 'Look, I must be dead – there's no blood.'[56]

This man wasn't mucking around trying to embarrass his mother-in-law in front of her friends from the tennis club. He genuinely believed himself to be dead. In the same way, another patient, a young woman, expressed guilt about drawing social security payments. She was worried that, being dead, she wasn't really eligible for her benefits. These patients suffer from the Cotard delusion, which some researchers think might be the result of a brain being even more excessive in its depersonalisation strategy. While to the depersonalisation patient the world seems distant or unreal, the Cotard patient may deny that the world even exists. While the depersonalisation disorder patient may feel as if their body no longer belongs to them, the Cotard patient may claim that parts of their body have rotted away altogether. And while the depersonalisation disorder patient may feel as *if* they were dead, the Cotard patient may actually believe it.

In these extreme cases of the Cotard delusion, so detached do patients feel from their feelings, thoughts, body and the world that nothing can persuade them that they are alive. One of the first Cotard patients to be reported, described by a psychiatrist in the 19th century, insisted upon being laid out on a shroud. She then began to fuss over the inadequate appearance of the linen, provoking the psychiatrist to complain irritably that 'even in death she cannot abstain from her female habit of beautifying herself ...'. The feeling of non-existence is inescapably compelling. Psychologists asked the young female Cotard patient with concerns about her eligibility for social security how she could feel heat and cold, feel her heart beat, feel when her bladder was full yet, despite this, nonetheless claim to be dead. The young woman cleverly replied that since she had these feelings despite being dead, they clearly could not be taken as good evidence that she was alive – a rebuttal that would possibly have stymied Descartes himself.

In fact, when Descartes famously wrote 'cogito, ergo sum', *cogito* referred not just to thinking, but to a rich variety of experiences, including emotions. Depersonalisation – in you, in depersonalisation disorder patients, in Cotard patients – suggests that when the brain turns down the volume on the emotions, your sense of self begins to slip away.

The balance that the sergeant major of the emotional brain has to achieve is a delicate one. Too much emotion and we wind up bawling over a ballpoint pen that someone has taken from us, detained in a secure psychiatric hospital, or paralysed with terror in the face of a few schoolchildren and several million *E. coli* bacteria. Yet if the emotional brain becomes too stingy with the emotions, the consequences can be no less devastating. As the chronically indecisive patient EVR demonstrates, remove the ability to use emotions as information and the simplest decision becomes irredeemably perplexing. Dampen down the emotions too much and we begin to lose grasp of our precious sense of self. And even when the sergeant major gets the balance about right, we are left mildly deluded about our opinions and judgments. Emotional aftermath from incidental circumstances – the gift of a cheap freebie, a spot of rain, the agitation of light exercise – can all colour our seemingly dispassionate views. Your emotional brain has its sweaty fingers in all the pies, from the shampoo you try to the morals you buy. Considering how often it enjoys the upper hand over your reasoning, better hope that your emotional brain is doing a reasonable job.

The Deluded Brain

A slapdash approach to the truth

When learned psychiatrists got together to brain-storm their way to an official description of delusions, they had a hell of a time coming up with a definition that didn't make a large proportion of the population instantly eligible for psychiatric services.[57] One can imagine the increasingly frustrated attempts to position appropriately the line between sanity and madness:

Dr A: So who would like to kick off with a definition of delusions?

Dr B: Can I suggest 'a false belief'?

Dr C: Wonderful! I shall instantly cure all of my paranoid patients by arranging for them to be persecuted.

Dr B: *If* you would be so kind as to let me finish, Dr

C? As I was saying, 'a false belief held despite evidence to the contrary'.

Dr C: Oh, I see. Such as, for example, your tenaciously held views on the beneficial effects of psychoanalysis for manic-depression?

Dr B: I hardly consider your article in the *Journal of Psychiatry* a convincing source of contrary evidence for my position, Dr C, if it is to that that you refer.

Dr A: Doctors, please! What about 'a false belief held despite incontrovertible and obvious evidence to the contrary'?

Dr B: Does it help, the question of evidence? I can't prove to my psychotic patients that the devil *isn't* transmitting thoughts into their head, any more than I can prove wrong the 150 million Americans who believe it possible for someone to be physically possessed by the devil.

Dr A: True. Or the 25 million Britons who believe in communication with the dead. But we can't allow everyone with a common or garden belief in the paranormal to be defined into madness – there simply aren't enough psychiatrists to cope.

Dr B: I think we'll just have to tack on something about delusions being beliefs that almost nobody else believes … I'm sorry, did you say something, Dr C?

Dr C: Oh, nothing.

Our beliefs range from the run-of-the-mill to the strikingly bizarre, yet many of them embrace their own share of deviancy from reality. Our first problem is that we are very poor scientists. All sorts of biases can slip in unnoticed as we form and test our beliefs, and these tendencies can lead us astray to a surprising degree. Of course, as we saw in 'The Vain Brain', and will see again in 'The Bigoted Brain', an ignoble agenda – the desire to see evidence for a belief we'd secretly prefer to hold – can wreak its prejudicing influence on our opinions. However, even when we genuinely seek the truth, our careless data collection and appraisal can leave us in woeful error about ourselves, other people, and the world. Then consider our susceptibility to strange experiences. After all, hallucinations, déjà vu, premonitions, depersonalisation, and religious experiences are not uncommon in the general population.[58] This is a perilous combination, and it's not yet clear exactly what it is that saves most of us from crossing the shady line that separates everyday delusions from the clinical variety.

Evidence of our deluded brains begins with a seemingly innocuous question: Are you happy with your social life? Or, to put it another way, are you unhappy with your social life?

Your answer, you may be surprised to learn, is astonishingly sensitive to which way the question is phrased. People asked if they are happy, rather than unhappy, with their social lives report greater satisfaction.[59] Responsibility for this peculiar irrationality in our self-knowledge lies with what is known as the 'positive test strategy'. As we contemplate that fascinating inner tangle of our attitudes, personality traits and skills, we ask our internal oracle questions to divine what we suppose to be the truth about ourselves. Am I happy with my social life? Do I want to stay married? Would I make a good parent? You then trawl through your store of self-knowledge searching for evidence that the hypothesis in question is correct. You remember that party you enjoyed last weekend. The touching interest your spouse takes in the small potatoes of your life. Your remarkable talent for manipulating balloons into the shape of animals.

Phrase the question the other way round, however, and your memory throws up a very different pile of evidence. Am I unhappy with my social life? Now you remember what bores you find most of your friends. Do I want a divorce? You think of that dreadful silent meal on your anniversary. Would I make a bad parent? Suddenly your unfortunate tendency to leave valuable possessions behind on public transport comes to mind. That's why people asked if they're happy (rather than unhappy) with their social lives believe themselves to be happier on that front. (The positive test strategy is also the reason you should never ask someone 'Don't you love me any more?')

We use the positive test strategy to test hypotheses about others as well as ourselves, with similarly distorting effects. Crucial decisions may fall one way or another as a consequence of something as trivial as which way round the question is phrased. People's deliberations about custody cases, for example, can yield very different outcomes depending on whether they are asked 'Which parent should have custody of the child?' or 'Which parent should be denied custody of the child?'[60] In this classic experiment, Parent A was moderately well equipped for custody in all respects: income, health, working hours, rapport with the child and social life. Parent B, in contrast, had a rather more sporadic parental profile. On the one hand, Parent B had an above average income and a very close relationship with the child. But on the other hand, this parent had an extremely active social life, a great deal of work-related travel, and minor health problems. When people were asked who should have custody of the child, they followed the positive test strategy of searching for evidence that each parent would be a good custodian. As a result, Parent B's impressive credentials with regard to income and relationship with the child shone out over Parent A's more modest abilities on these fronts, and nearly two-thirds of participants plumped for Parent B as the best custodian.

Ask who should be *denied* custody, however, and a very different picture emerges. The positive test strategy yielded evidence of Parent B's inadequacies as a guardian: the busy social and work life, and the health problems. By comparison, a positive test strategy search of Parent A's more pedestrian profile offered no strong reasons for rejection as a guardian. The result: the majority of participants decided to deny Parent B custody.

You may be relieved to be assured that the positive test strategy has an effect only if there is genuine uncertainty in your mind about the issue you are considering. It's not going to make much difference whether you ask a feminist if they approve of unequal pay for men and women, or whether they disapprove. Nonetheless, the implication of the positive test strategy research is rather worrisome, suggesting as it does that many difficult choices in our lives, based on our inferences about ourselves and others, might perhaps have swung the other way if we had only considered them from the opposite angle.

A second damaged tool in all of our personal scientific toolboxes is the brain software we use to spot correlations. Correlation is what put the warning messages on packets of cigarettes. There are plenty of 80 year olds puffing away on a couple of packs a day but, on the whole, the more you smoke the more likely it is that the Grim Reaper will scythe his way in your direction sooner rather than later. If *everyone* who smoked died from lung cancer then the tobacco companies might not have been able to kid on for so long that smoking was a harmless hobby. But because nature is messy and complicated, correlations are very difficult to spot 'by eye', and it took statistical analysis to pinpoint the relationship between smoking and cancer.

You may not want to blame your brain for not coming equipped with the full functionality of a statistical analysis program. However, you *may* want to get a little shirty about your brain's little habit of making up statistical results. Your brain has a sneaky tendency to 'see' correlations it expects to see, but that aren't actually there. This is called 'illusory correlation' and the classic demonstration of it in action was provided back in 1969, using the Rorschach inkblot test.[61] At that time, Rorschach's inkblots were very much in vogue as a diagnostic tool for psychoanalysts. The idea behind this infamous test is that what you see in the carefully designed splodges of ink reveals some well-hidden horror of your psyche to the psychoanalyst. While you are innocently spotting butterflies and faces, thinking it a pleasant ice-breaker before the real work begins, the psychoanalyst is listening to the sweet ker-CHING! of the therapy till.

Back in the 60s when this experiment took place, homosexuality was still regarded as a mental illness, and therapists had all sorts of ideas about what homosexuals tended to see in the inkblots. The experimenters surveyed 32 experienced clinicians, asking them what they had noticed in their homosexual clients when they used the inkblots. Almost half of the clinicians said that these patients tended to see 'anal content', to use the unhappily evocative phrase employed in the field. However, scientific research even at that time showed that there was no such relationship: homosexual men are no more likely to see butts in blots than heterosexuals. To try to understand why the clinicians were making this mistake, the Chapmans gave first-year psychology students some fake clinical experience. The students read through 30 fictitious case-notes, like the example overleaf. Each case-note showed first an inkblot, then what the patient claimed to have seen in the inkblot (in this example, 'horse's rear end'), and the patient's two chief emotional 'symptoms'. (Remember, we're back in the inglorious era when homosexuality was regarded as a mental illness.)

Note: For reasons of copyright, the above inkblot is not a genuine Rorschach inkblot and has been created for this book for illustration purposes only.

The case-notes were cleverly designed to ensure that, overall, there was absolutely no relationship between the 'symptom' of homosexual feelings and seeing something to do with bottoms in the blots. Yet when the Chapmans asked the students whether they'd noticed any relationship between homosexual tendencies and seeing certain sorts of things in the blots, over half of the students reported 'seeing' a correlation with rear-ends. The students saw the same illusory correlation as the clinicians. They saw what wasn't there. In fact, this mistaken belief persisted even when the case-notes were arranged such that homosexuals were *less* likely to report 'anal content' than straight clients.

This experiment should have had the clinicians blushing into their beards. (It was the dawn of the 70s and they were psychoanalysts: of course they had beards.) Despite their many years of professional experience, the clinicians turned out to be working with the same facile and erroneous hypothesis that first-year psychology students developed during a 30-minute experiment. The reason was illusory correlation. On the surface it seemed like a plausible hypothesis. Gay men talking about bottoms: who needs Dr Freud to work that one out? With a deceptively convincing hypothesis embedded in your skull, it is but one short step for your brain to start 'seeing' evidence for that hypothesis. Your deluded brain sees what it expects to see, not what is actually there. Treat with the greatest suspicion the proof of your own eyes.

A further problem with our beliefs, and the topic of the next chapter ('The Pigheaded Brain'), is the irrational loyalty that we show towards them. Once acquired, even the most erroneous beliefs enjoy an undeserved level of protection from rejection and revision.

So, what with our proclivity towards seeking evidence that supports whichever hypothesis we happen to be entertaining (the positive test strategy), our penchant for simply inventing supporting evidence (illusory correlation), and our pigheaded retention of beliefs, it becomes easy to see how our unsound scientific strategies can have unhappy consequences for the accuracy of the beliefs to which we are led. Yet these distortions pale into insignificance when stood beside clinical delusions. Thinking yourself a little less happy with your social life than you actually are is not in the same ballpark as believing yourself dead (the Cotard delusion). Falling prey to an illusory correlation between your moods and your menstrual cycle[62] simply does not compare with the delusional belief that your thoughts are being controlled by the devil. And misjudging your spouse's fitness to continue on in the role as your life companion does not hold a candle to the belief, known as the Capgras delusion, that your spouse (or other family member) has been replaced by an alien, robot, or clone.

The false beliefs of the delusional patient are simply of a different order of magnitude to our own modest misconceptions. Yet it has proved remarkably difficult to establish what the difference is between, say, the Capgras patient who is convinced that her husband has been replaced by a robot, and the person who goes no further than occasionally fantasising about the joys of a Stepford spouse. Until quite recently, the psychoanalytic crew were having a field day with the Capgras delusion. According to their way of looking at the delusion, it is subconsciously held feelings of ambivalence towards a family member that are helpfully resolved by the belief that the person has been replaced by an impostor.

Voila! A *bona fide* reason to no longer love your mother. However, recent progress in cognitive neuro-psychiatry has put a few spanners in the psychodynamic works.[63] For one thing, Capgras patients often show signs of brain injury, which suggests that it isn't simply their subconscious playing up. Moreover, some Capgras patients also claim that personal belongings have been replaced – and it's hard to describe convincingly the subconscious hatred a patient has towards his watch or, as in one curious case, a tube of Polyfilla.[64]

Then an exciting discovery was made: Capgras patients aren't emotionally aroused by familiar people.[65] Normally, when you see someone you know, your skin conductance response increases, showing that that person is of some emotional significance to you. But Capgras patients don't produce this emotional buzz. Could this be the key to their delusion? Some psychologists have suggested that it is. The Capgras patient recognises the person in front of them ('Well, it certainly *looks* like my husband …') but, because of brain injury, gets no emotional tingle from the experience ('… but it doesn't feel like my husband'). In order to explain this strange emotional lack, the patient concludes that the person in front of them must be an impostor of some sort.[66] In other words, at least part of the reason that you have never woken up one morning, looked at your husband, and then twitched open the nets in search of the spaceship he came in on is that your brain is intact. You may not be thrown into a fit of passion by his crazy bedhead hairstyle, but you will at least produce the minimally required level of sweat when you see his face.

But can this really be the whole story? The Capgras belief is so irrational, so impossible, so – let's just say it – nutty, that it's hard to understand why the patients themselves don't immediately reject as a ludicrous nonsense the idea that their husband or wife has been replaced by an alien. Especially since the patients themselves can be intelligently coherent, and well aware of how far their assertion strains credulity.[67] Nonetheless they politely maintain that, in their case, it just so happens to be true. What is it, then, that pushes delusional patients over the brink? One idea is that part of the problem for delusional patients is that they are even worse everyday scientists than we are. One hypothesis along these lines is that delusional patients 'jump to conclusions'.[68] Instead of sampling a decent amount of data before forming a belief, the delusional patient leaps foolhardily to their half-baked conclusion on the flimsiest of evidence. Intuitively, this makes sense. After all, how much evidence can the Capgras patient actually have for his claim that his wife has been replaced by a robot?

The classic test used to put to the proof the 'jumping to conclusions' hypothesis is known as the Beads Task.[69] Follow the instructions and take a turn yourself – if you dare.

Here are two jars of beads – A and B. Jar A has 85 white beads and 15 black beads. Jar B has 85 black beads and 15 white beads. Beads will be drawn from the same jar each time. Your task is to decide which jar the beads are being drawn from. You can see as many beads as you like to be completely sure which jar has been chosen.

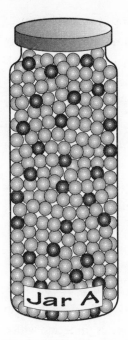

The list of beads drawn from the mystery jar is over-leaf. Place a thickish piece of paper behind this page. Then, when you're ready, turn over and slowly pull the piece of paper down until you can see the first bead. Keep on slowly pulling the cover sheet down until you have seen enough beads to be confident which jar they came from. Then count the number of beads you saw and turn to the next page.

REMINDER

JAR A: MOSTLY WHITE BEADS
JAR B: MOSTLY BLACK BEADS

BLACK BEAD

BLACK BEAD

BLACK BEAD

WHITE BEAD

BLACK BEAD

BLACK BEAD

BLACK BEAD

BLACK BEAD

BLACK BEAD

WHITE BEAD

WHITE BEAD

In these studies people generally ask for between three and four beads before they feel confident enough to say that the beads are being drawn from Jar B (you did choose Jar B, I hope?). It's probably close to the number of beads that you yourself chose. However, in the eyes of a statistician you would have been going on looking at bead after bead for a pathetically timid length of time. The probability of the bead being from Jar B after the first black bead is a whopping 85 per cent. After the second black bead, this increases to 97 per cent. At this point, the statistician impatiently waves the jars away exclaiming that they have seen enough. You and I, however, carry on to the next bead, and the next, just to get that additional tiny extra likelihood of being correct. People suffering from delusions, in contrast, request only about two beads before making their decision. In other words, they are better 'scientists' than we are.[70] Back to the drawing board.

But wait! In a study of all that can go wrong with reasoning, Professors Wason and Johnson-Laird describe the 'repetition, asseveration, self-contradiction, outright denial of the fact, and ritualistic behaviour' that they observed in a group of people whose reasoning was so poor, they fetched up as material for a book chapter bluntly entitled 'Pathology of Reasoning'.[71] This sounds promising; here's one of the tasks. Participants were told that the sequence of three numbers (called a triad) '2 4 6' fulfilled a simple relational rule chosen by the experimenter. The participants' task was to try to work out what the rule was by offering their own patterns of three numbers. After each triad they were told whether or not it conformed to the rule. People were told to announce their hypothesis about what the rule was only when they were confident that they were correct. The rule was that the numbers had to get bigger as they went along (or, as the professors preferred to put it, 'numbers increase in order of magnitude'). It could hardly have been simpler. (As Professor Johnson-Laird may well have remarked to his colleague, 'Elementary, my dear Wason.') Yet take a look at the tortured performance of the person who proffered three increasingly convoluted hypotheses before giving up in defeat nearly an hour later (a few examples of triads offered are given before the hypotheses):

8 13 15 [correct]

1 2031 2033 [correct]

'The rule is that the first and second numbers are random, and the third is the second plus two.'

4 5 7 [correct]

9 5 7 [incorrect]

263 364 366 [correct]

'The rule is that the first and second numbers are random, but the first is smaller than the second, and the third is the second plus two.'

41 43 42 [incorrect]

41 43 67 [correct]

67 43 45 [incorrect]

'The rule is that the second number is random, and either the first number equals the second minus two, and the third is random but greater than the second; or the third number equals the second plus two, and the first is random but less than the second.'

What did Professors Wason and Johnson-Laird make of this convoluted performance? 'It is not difficult to detect strong obsessional features …', they remark. 'He offers merely three formulations of [his conjecture about the rule] within a space of 50 minutes, and finally arrives at a complex disjunction which largely preserves the remnants of previous hypotheses. These are strong hints that his fertile imagination, and intense preoccupation with original hypotheses, has narrowed his field of appreciation to the point where he has become blind to the obvious.'

Well! Blind to the obvious, eh. Doesn't that just describe delusional patients to a T. They get it stuck into their heads that their wife is a cloned replacement, and nothing will persuade them otherwise. Have Wason and Johnson-Laird found the holy grail of a reasoning abnormality in patients with delusions? It certainly looks like it, but for one small problem. Not one of their participants was mentally ill. They were mentally healthy university students. In the particular example I described, the volunteer was a male science undergraduate at Stanford University.

In fact, on the whole, delusional patients tend to do just as well (or rather, just as badly) as we do on reasoning tests.[72] This has resulted in a rather cantankerous academic debate. Everyone agrees that delusional patients often have a very strange experience of which they must make sense: the Capgras patient has to explain why his wife no longer feels familiar; the Cotard patient has to account for her overwhelming detachment from her sense of self. But on one side of the debate there are the researchers who think it obvious that there must also be something odd about the reasoning abilities of somebody who can believe, for example, that they don't exist. How else could they entertain such a fantastical belief?[73] Yet others, in response, merely wave an expansive hand towards the bulky testimony to the sorry irrationality of the healthy brain and ask, what more is needed?[74]

The idea that we are no more rational than the pathologically deluded may not appeal greatly to our vanity, yet it remains an intriguing possibility. Take, for example, the delusion of control often suffered by patients with schizophrenia. These patients believe that their thoughts, actions and impulses are being controlled by an external force, such as an alien, or radar. Some researchers think that the problem lies in the patient's inability to keep tabs on his intentions: to brush his hair, stir his tea, pick up a pen.[75]

This means that he is no longer able to tell the difference between actions he has willed, and actions that are 'done to him'. Because he can no longer match an action with his intention to perform it, it feels as if it is externally caused. Struggling to explain this strange experience, the patient may come to believe that some external agent is now in command of him.

The question is, do you need some sort of peculiarity of reasoning to be able to accept that the idea that an alien is controlling your brain is a reasonable explanation of your experience? The jury is still out, but consider what I will call the 'alien hand' experiment.[76] The volunteers (normal, healthy Danes) had to track a target with a joystick, and they could see on a screen how they were doing. But on certain trials, unbeknown to them and by means of ingenious guile, the volunteers saw a false hand instead of their own. The hand moved in time with the volunteer's actual hand, but it was deliberately designed to miss the target. It didn't do quite what the volunteers were 'telling' their own hand to do. After the experiment, the volunteers were asked to explain their poor performance on the false hand trials. Here are some examples of the explanations suggested by the sane Danes:

'It was done by magic.'

'My hand took over and my mind was not able to control it.'

'I was hypnotised.'

'I tried hard to make my hand go to the left, but my hand tried harder and was able to overcome me and went off to the right.'

'My hand was controlled by an outside physical force – I don't know what it was, but I could feel it.'

Remember, these were normal, psychiatrically healthy people experiencing a slight and brief discrepancy between their motor commands and their perceptual experience. This is nothing in comparison with the continually discombobulating experiences of the patient with schizophrenia. Yet it was enough for at least some of the mentally healthy Danish participants to invoke the powers of hypnosis, magic and external forces, in order to explain the modest waywardness of a single appendage.

The fanciful explanations conjured up by the volunteers in the 'alien hand' experiment may seem surprising. Yet around half of the general, psychiatrically healthy population have faith in the powers of paranormal phenomena, such as witchcraft, voodoo, the occult or telepathy.[77] And why not alien forces? Half of the American public claims to believe that aliens have abducted humans. Presumably these 150 million people would have no reason to think that bodysnatching extra-terrestrials would draw the line at interfering with a Danish psychology experiment.[78]

The frequency of odd experiences in our everyday lives may go some way towards explaining the popularity of peculiar beliefs. As it turns out, strange experiences of the type suffered by clinically deluded patients are quite common in the general population. In one recent survey, mentally healthy participants were asked about odd experiences they might have had, and the 40 experiences that they were offered to pick from were based on actual clinical delusions.[79] For example, they were asked, 'Do your thoughts ever feel alien to you in some way?' and 'Have your thoughts ever been so vivid that you were worried other people would hear them?'. The average participant admitted to having had over 60 per cent of these 'delusional' experiences. What's more, one in ten participants reported *more* such experiences than did a group of psychotic patients who were actually suffering from pathological delusions. Combine these common strange experiences in the general population with the unfortunate irrationality of the healthy brain – its biased and unscientific approach to evaluating hypotheses – and you begin to understand the blurring of the line between pathological delusions and the normal deluded brain.

Despite our irrationality, despite the oddities of our experiences, most of us nonetheless manage to remain compos mentis. Yet it's still not clear what keeps us from falling over onto the wrong side of the line. Perhaps in some cases our strange experiences are less intense, less compelling, than those suffered by people who go on to develop full-blown clinical delusions.[80] Other times, perhaps, it is our personality, our emotional state, or our social situation that gives us greater strength to cope with odd experiences and that keeps us from seeking psychiatric help.[81] And sometimes, perhaps, our saving grace from a psychiatric diagnosis is nothing more than good luck that millions of others happen to share our delusion.

The Pigheaded Brain

Loyalty a step too far

On the matter of the correct receptacle for draining spaghetti, my husband demonstrates a bewildering pigheadedness. He insists that the colander is the appropriate choice, despite the manifest ease with which the strands escape through the draining holes. Clearly the sieve, with its closer-knit design, is a superior utensil for this task. Yet despite his apparent blindness to the soggy tangle of spaghetti in the sink that results from *his* method, my husband claims to be able to observe starchy molecules clinging to the weave of the sieve for weeks after it's been used for draining pasta. We have had astonishingly lengthy discussions on this issue – I have provided here merely the briefest of overviews – but after three years of marriage it remains unresolved. By which of course I mean that my husband hasn't yet realised that I'm right.

The longevity of these sorts of disagreements is well known to us all. I can confidently predict that until somebody invents a colander–sieve hybrid, we will not be able to serve spaghetti to guests. The writer David Sedaris, describing an argument with his partner over whether someone's artificial hand was made of rubber or plastic, also foresaw no end to their disagreement:

> 'I hear you guys broke up over a plastic hand,' people would say, and my rage would renew itself. The argument would continue until one of us died, and even then it would manage to wage on. If I went first, my tombstone would read IT WAS RUBBER. He'd likely take the adjacent plot and buy a larger tombstone reading NO, IT WAS PLASTIC.[82]

What is it about our brains that makes them so loyal to their beliefs? We saw in 'The Vain Brain' how our brains keep unpalatable information about ourselves from deflating our egos. The same sorts of tricks that keep us bigheaded also underlie our tendency to be pigheaded. The brain biases, discounts, misinterprets, even makes up evidence – all so that you can retain that satisfying sense of being in the right. It's not only our long-cherished beliefs that enjoy such devotion from our brains. Even the most hastily formed opinion receives undeserved safe-keeping from revision. It takes only a few seconds to formulate the unthinking maxim that 'a sieve should never get its bottom wet', but a lifetime isn't long enough to correct it. I think what I like most about everything you'll find in this chapter is that if you find it unconvincing, that simply serves to prove its point.

Our pigheadedness begins at the most basic level – what information we expose ourselves to. Who, for example, reads the *Daily Mail*? It's – well, you know – *Daily Mail* readers. People who like to begin sentences with 'Call me politically incorrect if you will, but …'. We don't seek refreshing challenges to our political and social ideologies from the world; we much prefer books, newspapers, magazines and people who share our own enlightened values. Surrounding ourselves with 'yes men' in this way limits the chances of our views being contradicted. Nixon supporters had to take this strategy to drastic levels during the US Senate Watergate hearings. As evidence mounted of political burglary, bribery, extortion, and other hobbies unseemly for a US President, a survey showed that the Nixon supporters developed a convenient loss of interest in politics.[83] In this way, they were able to preserve their touching faith in Nixon's suitability as a leader of their country. (In contrast, Americans who had opposed Nixon's presidency couldn't lap up the hearings quick enough.)

Our blinkered surveying of the world is only the beginning, however. Inevitably we are directly confronted with challenges to our beliefs, be it the flat-earther's view of the gentle downward curve of the sea at the horizon, a weapons inspector returning empty-handed from Iraq, or a plughole clogged with spaghetti. Yet even in the face of counter-evidence, our beliefs are protected as tenderly as are our egos. Like any information that pokes a sharp stick at our self-esteem, evidence that opposes our beliefs is subjected to close, critical and almost inevitably dismissive scrutiny. In 1956, a physician called Alice Stewart published a preliminary report of a vast survey of children who had died of cancer.[84] The results from her work were clear. Just one X-ray of an unborn baby doubled the risk of childhood cancer. A mere

24 years later, the major US medical associations officially recommended that zapping pregnant women with ionising radiation should no longer be a routine part of prenatal care. (Britain took a little extra time to reach this decision.)

Why did it take so long for the medical profession to accept that a dose of radiation might not be what the doctor should be ordering for pregnant women? A strong hint comes from several experiments showing that we find research convincing and sound if the results happen to confirm our point of view. However, we will find the exact same research method shoddy and flawed if the results fail to accord with our opinions.[85] For example, people either for or against the death penalty were asked to evaluate two research studies. One showed that the death penalty was an effective deterrent against crime, the other showed that it was not. One research design compared crime rates in the same US states before and after the introduction of capital punishment. The other compared crime rates across neighbouring states with and without the death penalty. Which research strategy people found the most scientifically valid depended mostly on whether or not the study supported their views on the death penalty. Evidence that fits with our beliefs is quickly waved through the mental border control. Counter-evidence, on the other hand, must submit to close interrogation and even then will probably not be allowed in.[86] As a result, people can wind up holding their beliefs even more strongly after seeing counter-evidence. It's as if we think, 'Well, if *that's* the best that the other side can come up with then I really must be right.' This phenomenon, called 'belief polarisation', may help to explain why attempting to disillusion people of their perverse misconceptions is so often futile.

It would be comforting to learn that scientists and doctors, in whose hands we daily place our health and lives, are unsusceptible to this kind of partisanship. I remember being briskly reprimanded by Mr Cohen, my A-level physics teacher, for describing the gradient of a line in a graph as 'dramatic'. Mr Cohen sternly informed me that there was no element of the dramatic in science. A fact was a plain fact, not some thespian prancing around on a stage. Yet a graph that contradicts the beliefs, publications and career of a scientist is anything but a 'plain fact'. Which is why scientific papers, identical in all respects but the results, are far more likely to be found to be flawed and unpublishable if the findings disagree with the reviewer's own theoretical viewpoint.[87]

Was this part of the reason that Alice Stewart's research on X-rays received such a stony reception? In her biography she recalls, 'I became notorious. One radiobiologist commented, "Stewart used to do good work, but now she's gone senile."'[88] Unfortunately for Stewart, a later study run by a different researcher failed to find a link between prenatal X-rays and childhood cancer. Even though the design of this study had substantial defects – as the researcher himself later admitted – the medical community gleefully acclaimed it as proof that they were right and Alice Stewart was wrong. The similarity of this story to the experimental demonstrations of biased evaluation of evidence is, well, dramatic. Eventually, of course, we got to the point we are at today, where a pregnant woman is likely to start rummaging in her handbag for her mace should an obstetrician even breathe the word 'X-ray' in her hearing. But it took a very long time to get there. By 1977, there was a huge amount of research showing a link between prenatal X-rays and childhood cancer. Yet the US

National Council on Radiation Protection remained stubbornly convinced that X-rays were harmless. They suggested an alternative explanation. It wasn't that radiation caused cancer. Ludicrous idea! No, the relationship between X-rays and cancer was due to the supernatural prophetic diagnostic powers of obstetricians. The obstetricians were X-raying babies they somehow *knew* would get cancer. This porcine hypothesis merits but one response: Oink, oink.

Beliefs don't simply possess an extraordinary capacity to twist your interpretation of evidence. More ominous still is the power of beliefs to create their own supporting evidence – the self-fulfilling prophecy. The placebo effect is probably the best-known example of this. Far less benign are the influences that other people's beliefs can have on you. Psychologists first of all directed their interest in the self-fulfilling prophecy upon themselves. Could a psychologist be unwittingly encouraging her volunteers to act in line with her beliefs about what should happen in the experiment? Psychologists found that they did indeed have this strange power over their experimentees.[89] Exactly the same experimental set-up yields reliably different results, depending on the beliefs of the researcher who is running the experiment and interacting with the participants. (In fact, even rats are susceptible to the expectations of experimenters.) Researchers can also unknowingly affect the health of participants in clinical drug trials. In a twist on the placebo effect, the *clinician's* beliefs about the effectiveness of a drug influence how effective it actually is. For this very reason, good clinical trials of drugs are now run 'double-blind'. Neither the patient nor the clinician knows what treatment the patient is getting.

Psychologists then got curious about whether the self-fulfilling prophecy might be silently at work outside the lab in the real world. In a notorious experiment, two psychologists turned their attention to the school classroom.[90] They gave a group of schoolchildren a fake test, which they claimed was a measure of intellectual potential. Then, supposedly on the basis of the test results, they told teachers that little Johnny, Eddy, Sally and Mary would be displaying an intellectual blossoming over the next few months. In fact, these children had been plucked randomly from the class list. Yet the teachers' mere expectation that these children would shortly be unfurling their mental wings actually led to a real and measurable enhancement of their intelligence. It's extraordinary to consider what a powerful impact a teacher's particular prejudices and stereo-types must have on your child. And the prophecy is not only self-fulfilling, it's self-perpetuating as well. When your son unwittingly fulfils his teacher's belief that 'boys don't like reading', that belief will become yet more comfortably established in the teacher's mind. There is something really very eerie about the power of other people's beliefs to control you with-out your knowledge. But there is little you can do to protect yourself against an enemy whose potency resides in its very imperceptibility. Of course you may sin as much as you are sinned against if that's any consolation, as you will see when we return to the self-fulfilling prophecy in 'The Bigoted Brain'.

As we've seen, the pigheaded brain and the vain brain use many of the same tricks to evade truth. The vain brain is protecting your self-esteem, your happiness, and your health. Are there any such bene-fits to your pigheadedness? Psychologists have pointed out that a modicum of obstinacy in relinquishing our beliefs is only sensible. After all, we would end

up in rather a flap if our beliefs continuously fluctu-
ated in response to every newspaper report or argument with an in-law. There's also a sense in which
our important beliefs are an integral part of who we
are. To bid a belief adieu is to lose a cherished portion of our identity.[91] Interestingly, people who have
recently indulged in extensive contemplation of
their best qualities (or been 'self-affirmed', to use the
cloying terminology of the literature) are more recep-
tive to arguments that challenge their strongly held
beliefs about issues like capital punishment and
abortion. By hyping up an important area of self-
worth, you are better able to loosen your grip on
some of your defining values. (Just loosen your grip,
mind. Not actually let go.) Effusive flattery dulls the
sword of an intellectual opponent more effectively
than mere logical argument.

It would be much more pleasant to leave it at
that: we're pigheaded, yes, but it's for good reasons.
However, research shows that our stubbornness is so
pernicious that even the most groundless and fledg-
ling belief enjoys secure residence in a pigheaded
brain. As a consequence, we are spectacularly vulnerable to our initial opinions and impressions. In a

classic demonstration of this, some volunteers were given a test of their 'social sensitivity'.[92] They read a series of pairs of suicide notes and for each pair they had to guess which note was genuine and which was a fake. Some volunteers were then arbitrarily told that their 'social sensitivity' performance was superior, others that it was inferior. A little later the experimenter debriefed the volunteers. The experimenter explained that the feedback they'd been given about their social sensitivity was made up, and that their supposed score had been randomly decided before they even walked into the lab. Any ideas the volunteers had developed about their proficiency in discriminating between genuine and fake suicide notes should have been abolished by the debriefing. After all, the evidence on which those beliefs were based had been entirely discredited. And yet, the volunteers continued to believe in their superior or inferior social sensitivity. When the experimenter asked the volunteers to guess how well they would actually do on this and other similar tasks, their answers reflected whether they had been given 'superior performance' or 'inferior performance' false feedback on the suicide notes task.

What is particularly remarkable about this experiment is that even people who were told that they were social clodhoppers carried on believing it. Even though their vain brains had been handed a *bona fide* rationale on which to restore their self-esteem, they continued to believe the worst about themselves. In a similar experiment, researchers gave high school students training in how to solve a difficult mathematical problem.[93] Half of the students watched a clear and helpful video presentation. The other half watched a deliberately confusing video presentation that left them floundering. Unsurprisingly, these latter students wound up feeling pretty crestfallen over their ham-handedness with numbers. This lack of confidence persisted even after the researchers showed them the clear video presentation, and explained that their poor maths performance was due to their bad instruction, not their actual ability. For even three weeks later, the students unfortunate enough to have watched the baffling video presentation were less likely to show interest in signing up for other similar maths classes. And so, possibly, the entire course of their future lives was changed.

Indeed, at this point you may be beginning to feel

uneasy stirrings about the ethics of psychology researchers giving false feedback – particularly negative feedback – to unsuspecting volunteers. The first chapter of this book ('The Vain Brain') was bulging with experiments in which unsuspecting volunteers were told something unpleasant about their personalities, skills, future prospects or health. To be sure, the experimenters always debriefed the hapless volunteers afterwards, but it looks as if debriefing alone isn't enough. The researchers in the suicide notes experiment discovered that normal debriefing procedures are hopelessly ineffective in correcting pigheadedly held beliefs. Only by painstakingly explaining the 'belief perseverance' phenomenon, and describing how it might affect the volunteer, were the experimenters able to leave their volunteers in the same psychological condition in which they found them. This is a little worrisome – although evidently not to psychology researchers. Of course, you can see it from a researcher's point of view. Yes, you tell some helpful person who has kindly agreed to help you in your research that, oh dear, they've made an embarrassingly poor effort on a test compared with almost everyone else who's ever passed through the lab. But then, probably less than an hour later, you clearly explain that what you told them wasn't true, that you didn't even trouble to mark their test. It's hard to credit that this might be insufficient to rid even the most self-doubting individual of any lingering doubts.

Clearly, however, normal debriefing *is* strangely inadequate. Why is it that beliefs take such an immediate and tenacious grasp of our brains? One answer is that our rich, imaginative and generally spurious explanations of things are to blame. You hear a rumour that a friend's teenager is pregnant. Discussing her dubious situation with a friend, you sadly call attention to the parents' regrettable insistence on treating adolescents as if they were adults, the *laissez-faire* attitude of the mother towards curfews, and the risqué clothes in which they let their daughter appear in public. In the face of such parental licence, the young woman's accident takes on a tragic inevitability. As a result, when you subsequently learn that the rumoured pregnancy concerned someone else's daughter, you find yourself thinking that it is only a matter of time before the slandered girl suffers the same misfortune. You may even comment, with the satisfying if misguided confidence of Cassandra, that 'There's no smoke without fire.' The initial belief recruits its own web of supporting evidence, derived from the facile causal explanations that we're so good at creating (and, let's be honest, are so much fun to indulge in). You can then take the initial fact away. The web of explanation is strong enough to support the belief without it.

In an experiment that simulated just this kind of gossipy social reasoning, volunteers were given a real clinical case history to read.[94] One case study, 'Shirley K.', was an anxious young mother and housewife whose history included such misfortunes as divorce, the suicide of her lover, her father's death, and the eventual commitment of her mother to a mental institution. Some of the volunteers were then asked to put themselves in the role of a clinical psychologist who had just learned that Shirley K. had subsequently committed suicide. They were asked what clues, if any, they found in Shirley K.'s life story that might help a psychologist explain or predict her suicide. The volunteers embraced this task with enthusiasm. They easily came up with plausible sounding hypotheses; for example, that the suicide of her lover was 'a model that led her to take her own life'. Once the volunteers had done this they were told that in fact nothing was known about Shirley K.'s future life. The suicide they had been asked to explain was only hypothetical. However, the web of explanation had been spun. When asked how likely it was that Shirley K. *would* in fact commit suicide, the volunteers rated this as being much more likely than did another group of people who had not been asked to explain the hypothetical suicide. In fact, even people told beforehand that the suicide didn't actually happen nonetheless found their theories about why a suicide *might* have occurred so convincing that they, too, pegged Shirley K. as a high suicide risk.

A later study showed just how crucial these sorts of speculations are in helping to bolster a belief. In a variation of the experiment in which volunteers were given made-up information about their ability to tell the difference between genuine and fake suicide notes, volunteers were told (as in the original experiment) that their performance was either superior or inferior.[95] As before, some of the volunteers were then left free to run wild with theories to explain their supposed level of 'social sensitivity'.

When then told that the feedback they had been given had been fabricated, these volunteers nonetheless continued to cling to their newfound belief about their social abilities (just as did the volunteers in the original experiment). The false feedback they had received was by then just a small part of the 'evidence' they had for their opinion regarding their social sensitivity. Something very different happened, however, with a second group of volunteers who were prevented from searching for explanations for their allegedly good or bad performance on the task. These volunteers were immediately commanded to keep themselves busy in an absorbing task. Denied the opportunity to rummage in their brains for other 'evidence' to support their flimsy belief about their social sensitivity, these volunteers sensibly abandoned the belief as soon as they learnt that it was based on lies. It's our irresistible urge to play amateur psychologist that makes us so vulnerable to our initial beliefs, no matter how bluntly the facts they were based on may be discredited. It's human nature to try to explain everything that happens around us, perhaps as a way to make life seem less capricious.

Our susceptibility to first impressions is compounded by another, rather endearing, human failing. We are credulous creatures who find it easy to believe, but difficult to doubt. The problem, according to the 17th-century philosopher Spinoza, is that we believe things to be true as a matter of course. As Spinoza's present-day champion, psychologist Daniel Gilbert, has put it, 'you can't not believe everything you read'. Of course we are not lumbered with our gullible beliefs for ever, or even for very long. However, it is only with some mental effort that we can decide that they are untrue. Our natural urge – our default position – is to believe. This may be because, in general, people speak the truth more often than not. It's therefore more efficient to assume that things are true unless we have reason to think otherwise.

But there is a problem with this system. If your brain is too busy with other things to put in the necessary legwork to reject a porkie pie, then you're stuck with that belief. Advertisers and car salesmen will be delighted to learn that incredulity really is hard work for us, or so research suggests. If your brain is distracted or under pressure, you will tend to believe statements that you would normally find rather dubious.[96] In fact, you may even find yourself believing things you were explicitly told were untrue. In one demonstration of this failure to 'unbelieve', volunteers read from a computer screen a series of statements about a criminal defendant (for example, 'The robber had a gun').[97] Some of the statements were false. The volunteers knew exactly which ones they were, because they appeared in a different colour of text. For some of the volunteers, the untrue statements made the crime seem more heinous, whereas for others the false testimony offered mitigating circumstances for the crime. At the same time that the volunteers were reading the statements, a string of digits also marched across the computer screen. Some of the volunteers had to push a button whenever they saw the digit '5'. Banal though this may seem, doing this uses up quite a lot of mental resources. This meant that these volunteers had less brain power available to mentally switch the labelling of the false statements from the default 'true' to 'false'. These busy volunteers were much more likely to misremember false statements as true. What's more, this affected how long the volunteers thought the criminal should serve in prison. For example, when the false statements unfairly exacerbated the severity of the crime, it made a big difference to the criminal whether he was being judged and tried by a distracted or an attentive volunteer. The distracted volunteers sentenced him to prison for almost twice as long a stretch.

Indeed, if your reputation is under examination, the gullible brains of others can put you in serious jeopardy. Because of our bias towards belief, we are particularly susceptible to innuendo. In a simulation of media election coverage, volunteers read a series of headlines about political candidates, and then gave their impressions of each of the politicians.[98] Unsurprisingly, headlines such as 'BOB TALBERT ASSOCIATED WITH FRAUDULENT CHARITY' left Talbert's reputation in tatters. Astonishingly, though, the headline 'IS BOB TALBERT ASSOCI-ATED WITH FRAUDULENT CHARITY?' was just as damaging. And if you're thinking of entering the public eye yourself, consider this: even the headline 'BOB TALBERT NOT LINKED WITH FRAUDU-LENT CHARITY' was incriminating in the eyes of the readers. Denials are, after all, nothing more than statements with a 'not' tagged on. The bit about 'Bob Talbert' and 'fraudulent charity' slips into our brains easily enough, but the 'not' isn't somehow quite as effective as it should be in affecting our beliefs. We are suckers for innuendo, even – as the study went on to show – when it comes from a disreputable source like a tabloid.

For any defendant under scrutiny in the courtroom, the beliefs of gullible brains are, of course, of crucial significance. Remember the joke circulating prior to the O.J. Simpson trial?

Knock, knock.
Who's there?
O.J.
O.J. who?
You're on the jury.

Pre-trial publicity is usually very bad news for a defendant whose future liberty or even life depends on the machinations of twelve pigheaded brains.[99] Perhaps because of our susceptibility to innuendo and even denials, media reports of crime encourage a pro-prosecution stance in jurors. It has been shown that the more a person knows about a case before the trial, the more guilty they think the defendant. Grisly media coverage aggravates the 'lock him up' attitude even further, even though the brutality of a crime obviously has no bearing whatsoever on whether or not that particular defendant is guilty. A juror who wallows in pre-trial publicity skews Justice's scales against the defendant, and the pigheaded brain that then biases, distorts and even makes up evidence to support this belief in the defendant's guilt certainly won't help to restore the balance.

So since the ramifications of our pigheadedness spread so much wider, and are so much more serious than controversy over the correct method for decanting spaghetti, is there anything we can do about it? At this point, psychology texts like to make a few half-hearted suggestions as to how we can combat the mulish tendencies of our minds. 'Entertain alternative hypotheses', we are urged. 'Consider the counter-evidence.' The problem of course is that we are convinced that we are already doing this; it's simply that the other guy's view is absurd, his arguments laughably flimsy. Our pigheadedness appears to be irredeemable. It is a sad fact that the research bears out the newspaper columnist Richard Cohen, who wrote that 'The ability to kill or capture a man is a relatively simple task compared with changing his mind.'[100]

My husband would do well to bear that in mind, come dinnertime.

The Secretive Brain

Exposing the guile of the mental butler

I remember my husband waking up one morning exclaiming, 'I had a dream last night!' This was quite an event, since my husband generally claims never to dream. He clearly expected me to show an interest: if not professionally then at least in my role as spouse. Certainly as a psychologist – indoctrinated to value only strictly scientific methods – I was entirely unequipped to offer my husband a Freudian analysis of his slumberous labours. The name Freud was not one mentioned often in the psychology department I attended as an undergraduate. Indeed, it was rumoured that the dusty collected works of Freud on the library shelves were wired to a generator. Anyone misguided enough to touch them would receive an enlightening electric shock – that popular educational tool of the experimental psychologist. Yet although I stand firmly in the camp of those who think 'Penis envy? Puh-*lease*', there is something tantalising about the promise offered by dreams, to reveal the secret machinations that go on below the paper-thin surface of the conscious mind. Which is why, despite myself, I felt a little thrill of excitement in response to my husband's announcement. Here at last was an unprecedented opportunity to take a peek at the uncensored ruminations of my husband's hidden mind. Thus it was that I found myself asking him to tell me all about his dream.

'I dreamed that we had an argument', he said proudly.

'Interesting', I replied thoughtfully. 'We had an argument last night.'

'Yes, my dream was almost exactly the same. God, I was mad. Do you want some tea?'

And there ended my brief psychoanalytic journey of discovery into my spouse's unconscious mind.

Fortunately, psychoanalysis is no longer the only route available into the covert portion of our mind. Over the past few decades social psychologists have been getting very interested in this aspect of our mental life, and what it's up to. Their research shows that there's both good news and bad news. The good news is that the unconscious isn't, as it's often billed, merely the boxing ring for psychic struggles. The unconscious mind works hard, efficiently and tirelessly on your behalf. One prominent social psychologist refers to it as the 'mental butler' who tends silently to our needs and desires, without us even having to trouble to ring the bell.[101] With the grunt work covered, the conscious mind is left at leisure to ponder life goals, make important decisions and generally run the show. Or does it? The bad news is that delegation always comes at a cost to control. When you hand over a job to your willing unconscious, you can never be quite sure how it's being done.

Actually, that's not the bad news. I just didn't want to break it to you too suddenly, while you were still glorying in the metaphor of your conscious self as master of the manor lording it over your staff of unconscious mental processes. The real bad news is that even our relatively rare moments of conscious choice may be nothing but an illusion. Like the hapless toff Bertie Wooster, who is but putty in the hands of his scheming butler Jeeves, recent research suggests that the hand that polishes the shoes walks the feet. You only *think* you're in charge of where you're going.

However, the unconscious – like Jeeves – is as indispensable as it is devious. Everyday activities, like walking and driving, perfectly illustrate the importance of being able to delegate responsibility to the unconscious mind. I recently observed my toddler son learning how to walk. As a twelve month old, it was an activity requiring the utmost concentration. No other business – receiving a proffered toy, taking a sip of water, or surveying the pathway ahead for obstacles – could be conducted at the same time. Imagine if this carried on throughout life: passers-by on the street would plop clumsily to their bottoms should you distract them for an instant by asking for directions. But fortunately, the unconscious gradually takes over. The previously tricky aspects of walking – balancing upright, moving forward, the whole left-foot-right-foot routine – become automatic and mentally effortless. Once a skill becomes the domain of the unconscious mind, we free up our conscious thought for other matters. The learner driver is a poor conversationalist because his conscious mind is fully taken up with the complexities of steering, changing gears and indicating. As driving becomes automatic, precious conscious thought becomes available again.

And conscious thought *is* a precious and limited resource. It's not just because it's a stream rather than a tributary of consciousness, limiting you to a single line of inner dialogue at any one time. The part of our consciousness that controls what we do – our will – gets tired surprisingly easily, it turns out. Even rather modest exertions of the will leave you in a weakened state so far as subsequent acts of volition are concerned. For example, hungry volunteers were left alone in a room containing both a tempting platter of freshly baked chocolate chip cookies, and a plate piled high with radishes.[102] Some of the volunteers were asked to sample only the radishes. These peckish volunteers manfully resisted the temptation of the cookies and ate the prescribed number of radishes. (The effort of will this required was splendidly demonstrated by several participants who were spotted, through a secret two-way mirror, picking up cookies and holding them up to their noses in order to inhale their aroma longingly.) Other, more fortunate, volunteers were asked to sample the cookies. In the next, supposedly unrelated part of the experiment, the volunteers were asked to try to solve a difficult puzzle. The researchers weren't interested in whether the volunteers solved it. (In fact, it was unsolvable.) Rather, they wanted to know how long the volunteers would persist with it. Their self-control already depleted, volunteers forced to snack on radishes persisted for less than half as long as people who had eaten the cookies, or – in case you should think that the chocolate cookies offered inner strength – other volunteers who had skipped the eating part of the experiment altogether.

It's not only resisting temptation that the conscious mind finds exhausting, as further experiments showed. Other duties of the volitional self – making simple decisions and controlling emotions, for example – also left people's wills sadly enfeebled. Afterwards, they quickly gave up on taxing puzzles, compared with people whose wills were fresh and unused. 'Ego depletion', as the researchers call it, may also explain why it's so hard to switch off the television after a hard day at work, regardless of how appalling the programme is. In a final experiment, some volunteers were given a highly mentally demanding task to do – the psychology lab equivalent of air traffic control. The other volunteers were used more like factory workers – their job was so repetitive and easy that it quickly became automatic. Then the volunteers watched a video, which they could stop at any time. The film challenged even the very worst of television viewing – it was an unchanging shot of a blank white wall with a table and computer equipment in the foreground. Drained by their Herculean task in the first part of the experiment, the air traffic controllers found themselves slumped inertly in front of the TV screen for much longer than the factory workers, too sluggish to summon up the will to press a buzzer to end the show.

All in all, your conscious you is just one pair of hands – and a weedy pair at that – which is why it needs so much help from the mental downstairs. Of course there's nothing particularly secretive or sinister about the idea of the conscious will demanding 'Home, James' and the unconscious following the order by smoothly taking over the routine of driving.

But what if the unconscious could automate the very act of willing, setting itself off in the pursuit of a goal without a conscious command from above?[103] The unconscious has been caught in this very act by recent research. If you are an experienced driver, a curve in the road triggers the unconscious to adjust the steering wheel without you even having to think about it. You might see the curve, but you don't notice the automatic effect it has on your steering. In a similar way, as we become experienced navigators of the social highway, the people and situations we encounter automatically trigger our unconscious to adjust our social steering in line with well-practised goals, without us even realising.

Our unconscious is particularly easily sparked off in this way by people, because our relationships with others are such hotbeds of motivations and goals. And since no chapter on the unconscious, however modern in its approach, would be complete without mention of mothers, we will take the worthy aim to 'make mother proud' as an example of an 'inter-personal goal'. If this is one of your goals (and I certainly hope it is) then your unconscious will not have failed to notice that when you find yourself thinking 'But what would mother say?' you strive to be and do better. So what the helpful unconscious does is to automatically set you the goal of going that extra mile, whenever anything in your situation reminds it of your mother. You, in the meantime – the conscious you, that is – are completely unaware that you're acting under the influence of a hidden agenda. In a demonstration of this, researchers recruited volunteer students who – months and months before – had been asked to write down the sorts of goals they had with respect to their mothers.[104] The volunteers were chosen so that about equal numbers did and did not have the goal of making their mother proud.

The researchers then poked the unconscious into automatically activating mother-related goals in some of the volunteers. They did this by 'priming' the 'mother schema', to use the technical terms. Schemas make up the filing system of your mind. Cognitive psychologists think that just about everything we learn about the world is neatly tidied away into a schema. I like to think of a schema as a big bed full of slumbering brain cells. All the brain cells in the bed represent a different part of the schema. So, for example, in the schema for dogs you'll find brain cells that – when active and awake – point out that dogs have four legs. Then there are the neurons that hold the information that dogs bark, neurons that remind you that dogs have hair, and all the neurons for just about everything else you know about the concept of dogs. And they're all tucked up in the same bed.

'Priming' a schema is like shaking a few of the brain cells awake. Because they're all snuggled up cosily in bed, waking one group of brain cells disturbs the sleep of all the others in the bed, and makes them more likely to wake up. And brain cells that are on the verge of wakefulness are much more likely to answer the call of the conscious than are brain cells sleeping undisturbed in another schema bed. (For example, researchers primed the 'Asian' schema in some volunteers by using an Asian experimenter to present a word completion task.[105] For the other volunteers, the experimenter was white. The task was to make words from fragments such as 'POLI_E' and 'S_Y'. The volunteers whose Asian schemas were primed by the Asian experimenter were more likely to come up with words from the Asian schema, like 'POLITE' and 'SHY', rather than, say, 'POLICE' and 'SKY'.)

To return to our 'make mother proud' experiment, the researchers primed the mother schema in some of the volunteers by asking them several questions about their mother: how old she was when she got married, hobbies, political preferences, and so on. In other words, they shook awake all the brain cells involved with information about 'MOTHER: MAJOR LIFE EVENTS, INTERESTS AND VALUES'. The researchers knew that this would also disturb the brain cells concerned with 'MOTHER: GOALS PERTAINING TO', which would all be lying somewhere in the same bed. The 'unprimed' volunteers were instead asked questions about themselves; their mother schema remained untouched. Next, all the volunteers were asked to have a go at a 'verbal skills' task, which involved generating as many words as they could in five minutes from a set of seven letters. How the volunteers did on the task depended both on whether they had the goal to make mother proud, and whether their mother schemas were primed. Volunteers who wanted to make their mother proud *and* had had their mother schema activated outperformed all of the other groups.

Don't think, however, that these volunteers were

consciously thinking, 'I must do well so I can tell Mum about this and make her proud of me.' The volunteers were quizzed carefully afterwards, and none realised that answering questions about their mother might have influenced how they did on the verbal skills task. Rather, it was the helpful uncon- scious – while shaking part of the mother schema awake in the first part of the experiment – that had also jostled the 'make mother proud' goal into action, influencing how hard the volunteer worked on the word generating task.

Indeed, proof that the unconscious is truly acting off its own bat (and not in response to a conscious decision to try harder) comes from priming experi- ments in which conscious awareness is bypassed altogether. In subliminal priming, a picture or word (for example, the word 'mother') is flashed up too briefly for you to become consciously aware of it, but long enough so that the quicker unconscious notices it. (About one tenth to one half of a second does the trick.) Subliminally priming volunteers has just the same sort of effect as the priming in the 'make mother proud' experiment. In one such experiment, for example, some volunteers were subliminally primed with the word 'father', then took an analytic reasoning test.[106] Afterwards, they were asked if it was important to their father that they, the volunteer, be a good analytic reasoner. Among the volunteers who said yes, it made a big difference whether or not they had been subliminally flashed with the word 'father' before the reasoning test. Father-primed volunteers significantly outdid their unprimed peers. Although they were completely oblivious to the surreptitious paternal flickering, it still had the power to make them work harder on the task.

What these and many other similar experiments show is that seemingly trivial things in our environment may be influencing our behaviour. Dormant goals are triggered without our even realising. It's not that we're necessarily unaware of the stimulus itself (as in the 'make mother proud' experiment). However, we are oblivious to the effect that it is having on our behaviour. Without our knowledge, we suddenly begin to pursue a goal that has been set off by some seemingly innocuous event. For example, if someone quizzes you about a good friend before asking you for a favour, you will be more willing to help them. This is because thinking about friends unconsciously primes the goal to help, so one experiment found.[107] Seemingly incidental events and objects appear to have dark powers over our behaviour, and the speculation begins where the experiments stop. Is that charming photo of your family on the desk at work imperceptibly encouraging you to head home earlier? If you have a deadline coming up, should you replace it with a portrait of your boss instead? What about that stapler; what's it up to? Looks innocent enough, but who knows what riot of motives it may be stirring in your brain.

Okay, the stapler is probably guiltless. But there are countless other suspects (the letter from your mother on the doormat, the song you heard on the radio on the way to work, maybe even that dead pigeon on the pavement), all of which may be changing the course of your life in their own, modest little way. And the unconscious doesn't stop at the willy-nilly firing up of goals, which are at least motives to which you subscribe. Any sort of schema can be primed. And when it is, our behaviour changes to fit with the schema. In one of the first extraordinary demonstrations of this phenomenon, volunteers had to unscramble several sentences in which the words were in the wrong order.[108] For some of the volunteers, the sentences used words related to the stereotype of old people: *wrinkle, bitter, knits, forgetful, stubborn,* and so on. The rest of the volunteers unscrambled sentences with only neutral words. The point of this was to prime the 'elderly schema' in the first group of volunteers, and to see what effect this had on their behaviour. So once the volunteers had finished the task and gathered up their belongings, the researcher thanked them, showed them to the door, and pointed out the lift at the end of the hall. A confederate lurking in the hallway then secretly timed how long the volunteers took to walk down the corridor. The volunteers who had rearranged words related to old people actually behaved like stooped old frost-tops themselves on the journey to the lift, walking significantly more slowly than the other volunteers.

As you might imagine, this generous propensity of your unconscious to invite any old schema knocking on the back door to come on in and join the party can be a good thing or a bad thing. It all depends on the schema. Volunteers primed with the schema of professors – a supposedly intelligent and knowledgeable breed – stormed their way to success at Trivial Pursuit, compared with volunteers not so benefited by priming.[109] But prime volunteers with the football hooligan schema instead, and Trivial Pursuit meltdown is what ensues. Dust off the 'polite' schema in people's brains, and the majority will wait patiently for more than ten minutes without interrupting the experimenter's mundane conversation with another student. Kindle the 'rudeness' schema instead, and most people will butt in long before ten minutes have passed.[110]

As if this mental mayhem weren't already enough to contemplate, do we also need to worry about our promiscuous unconscious being wooed by shameless subliminal marketing campaigns? Many people have heard of the nefarious début of subliminal priming made in the world of advertising back in the 1950s. James Vicary, the executive of a failing advertising company, claimed to have sky-rocketed coke and popcorn sales at cinemas by subliminally flashing 'DRINK COKE' and 'EAT POPCORN' messages at unsuspecting cinema-goers. It turned out to be a hoax – there had been no secret messages. Vicary was right not to have bothered: subliminal advertising didn't actually seem to have any real effects on people's attitudes towards products, or their buying behaviour.[111]

However, advertisers hadn't then fully mastered the tricky technical side of successful subliminal priming (for example, you need many flashes of the prime rather than just a few, and single words work better than sentences).[112] Social psychologists are becoming disturbingly successful at catching the 'consumer unconscious'. Using up-to-date priming techniques, they can influence people's attitudes towards advertised products. Volunteers subliminally flashed with a happy face before being offered a fruit-flavoured drink rated the concoction tastier, drank more of it, and were even willing to pay double the price for it, compared with volunteers flashed with angry faces.[113] In another experiment, volunteers subliminally primed with words to do with thirst thought that the thirst-quenching 'SuperQuencher' drink sounded superior to the energy-giving 'PowerPro' beverage. They also drank more of it, compared with volunteers not primed in this way.[114] However, in both experiments the volunteers had to be thirsty in order for the priming to work. Priming had no effect at all on volunteers who came pre-quenched. You heard it here first: when the new wave of underhand advertising begins, be sure to visit the cinema only when sated and slaked to the gills.

However gloomy all this may sound, be cheered that your unconscious is not entirely defenceless against unwanted influences. However, it needs a helping hand from your conscious. Remember that goals – acted on over and over in particular situations – come to be automatically set off by cues in the environment. This can be exploited to your great advantage in order to help noble and worthy goals triumph over base and shameful temptations. Your unconscious, despite everything, is still *your* unconscious. If you are disciplined about resisting temptation whenever it arises, then sooner or later your unconscious will reward you by joining the battle on your behalf. The tempting situation itself automatically triggers the goal to resist the temptation. This helpful trick can even stop you from eating chocolate, and here's the experiment to prove it.[115] First of all, researchers found themselves a group of women students who were all at least a little 'ooh, I shouldn't eat that' about food. One at a time, each woman was taken into a small office strewn with magazines and other props, carefully chosen to set the woman's unconscious working in a particular way. In the 'diet prime' office, the surfaces were covered with magazines about exercise and dieting, with flyers for weight watching classes pinned to the walls. Other women were led into the 'temptation prime' office. Here, the magazine of choice was *Chocolatier*, with various chocolate-based food items left lying around the office for good measure. For a third group of women, who were being used as a boring control group, the magazines were about economics or geography. The volunteer sat in the office while she did a computer task and then – oh so casually – was asked to select either a Twix bar or an apple, as thanks for her participation in the experiment.

Nearly two-thirds of the women bombarded with messages about dieting chose the apple. This showed impressive restraint over the norm, since nearly two-thirds of the women from the control group (who saw the economics and geography magazines) chose the Twix. The unobtrusive priming of the diet schema successfully tempered these women's natural tendency to choose the chocolate. What then was the effect of priming temptation, seemingly the opposite of the 'diet prime' condition? Remarkably, these women showed an abstemiousness equal to that of the 'diet prime' group. Because these women were used to gastronomic self-denial, the tempting images of the indulgent magazine and the chocolatey snacks automatically and unconsciously triggered the goal to restrain eating, and squelched the fleeting allure of short-term gratification: hoorah!

But don't forget that the conscious has to put in the legwork first. Your unconscious starts to pull its weight only once you have a solid history of resisting temptation through conscious effort behind you. You can't go around throwing sweeties down your gullet and expect the unconscious to get the right idea. This could be part of the reason why sublimi-nal self-help tapes don't work:[116] it takes conscious effort to reverse our bad habits. And unfortunately, as we've already seen from the 'ego depletion' exper-iments, there is only so much willpower to go round. If you use it all up resisting the chocolate cake then you will be especially vulnerable if another tempta-tion comes hot on its heels. Well, no one ever said that resisting temptation was easy. (Except the purveyors of subliminal self-help tapes, of course.)

At this point, we have learned a few disturbing facts about our unconscious. Nonetheless, its description as a 'mental butler' still seems reasonably apt. The unconscious takes a few liberties here and there, but it's basically on your side and – most important of all – you're more or less in charge. You think 'I'll take a shower', and then you take a shower. You think 'I'll go upstairs now' and lo, there you are, trotting upstairs. You think 'I shall move my right index finger and tap it on the desk' and – tap! – there your finger submits to the command. Your fingers, like all your limbs and appendages, are servants of the masterful conscious will. All day, every day, we decide to do things that – save interruption or distraction – we then do. It's obvious to the meanest intelligence that it is the conscious will that makes things happen.

But is that really the chain of command, or do we just think that it is? After all, we know that our bodies do sometimes submit to commands to which our conscious selves can't possibly lay claim. Consider the hand that flies off the hot saucepan handle before we even feel the pain, or the foot that slams on the brake before we consciously register the traffic hazard ahead. These reflexes are not preceded by any conscious decision, and so we are happy to gift the initiation of these reflexes to our unconscious mind. But just suppose for a moment that there is a place in our mind we know nothing about – call it the secret commander – that spends its day sending ideas to our conscious mind. 'Tell it to think "I'll tap my right index finger now"', the secret commander shouts, and off the message goes up to the conscious. In the meantime, the neuronal grunt workers get going obeying the secret commander by arranging the finger tap itself. From *your* point of view – knowing nothing about the secret commander – the order of proceedings seems to be:

1. Think 'tap finger'.
2. Finger taps.

To us, it seems obvious that the thought caused the action, just as a ball hitting a vase is what causes it to topple off the mantelpiece. But the actual course of events in our little imagined scenario is quite different. A mysterious unconscious process (the secret commander) caused the thought 'tap finger' and set the finger tap in motion. But because we know nothing about the mental activity that took place before we had the great idea to tap our finger, we very reasonably infer that our finger tapped because we willed it to be so.[117]

You might concede that this crazy idea – that our conscious will is a misguided delusion – is logically possible. Yes, it could happen, in theory. But why on earth should we believe it? Is there any reason to think that conscious will *isn't* actually what makes things happen?

To answer this question, we have to examine the simple process of moving one's finger in more detail than you ever thought possible. In a momentous experiment by a researcher called Benjamin Libet, volunteers made spontaneous, willed finger movements.[118] This was nothing very new or exciting for the volunteers: just the same old 'Think "move finger", finger moves' sequence. Libet, in the meantime, was busy taking very precise measurements. For starters, he immediately detected finger movements using a muscle movement sensor strapped to the volunteer's finger. As a matching accessory, the volunteer's head was encased in scalp electrodes that picked up brain activity. Libet found that about half a second before a person's finger moved, there was a little flurry of brain activity, called the 'readiness potential'. This flurry wasn't anything to do with implementing the actual finger movement: it wasn't the mundane but necessary instructions to get that finger up in the air. (That came later, right before the movement, in the motor control area of the brain.) What Libet was seeing when the readiness potential took place was the mighty command 'Move finger' itself.

The big question for Libet was where this command came from: conscious will, or the secret commander? Was the readiness potential a bunch of brain cells firing as the conscious decision to raise a finger came to fruition? Or did it correspond to the clandestine activities of the secret commander? The answer was in the timing. Libet asked his volunteers to report, for each finger movement, when exactly they became aware of having the conscious urge to perform the finger movement. The volunteers did this using a specially designed clock with very small time intervals; they were carefully trained to observe where the clock hand was at the moment they had the conscious urge to move.

And here's the remarkable thing. The volunteers didn't consciously experience the will to move their finger until more than a third of a second *after* the readiness potential. In other words, the unconscious brain was already busy preparing for the finger movement well before the idea occurred to the volunteer's consciousness. (You might think that this was just because the volunteers were a little slow at relating their awareness of their intention to move with the position of the clock hand. To make sure that this wasn't the case, in another series of trials Libet stimulated the volunteers' hands and asked them to report, using the same clock, when they felt the sensation. Because Libet knew exactly when their hands had been stimulated, he could work out the delay involved in using the clock. Even allowing, generously, for this error, the readiness potential still came well before the conscious intention.) This astonishing finding – that the brain can be busy preparing for intentions you haven't yet had – leaves us with the mysterious question of who – or what – ordered the finger to move? It couldn't have been conscious will. Was it our hypothetical secret commander?

The possibility that conscious will is an illusion challenges our sense of free will: the feeling that we are indeed masters of our destinies. It forces us to wonder if perhaps our lives are, as William James so poetically put it, nothing more than the 'dull rattling off of a chain that was forged innumerable ages ago'. Fortunately, freedom of will – if indeed a conceit – is such a compelling one that it's easy enough to slip back into falling for the trick. Even philosophers, who have a tendency to dwell on these sorts of things, generally go happily about their everyday lives without thinking twice about secret commanders and the rattling chains of foregone conclusions. There may well be a secret commander masterminding our every thought and deed, but at least he's discreet about it.

I hope you've enjoyed this tour into the unconscious mind. Forget Freud, forget dreams, forget stretching out on a comfy leather sofa: cognitive psychology is the new spyhole into the psyche. (You may also wish to note that the cost of this entire book would barely buy you a minute of psychoanalysis.) Yet despite all of the astonishing discoveries that have been made about the unconscious in the last few decades, we should not lose our humility. Never forget that your unconscious is smarter than you, faster than you, and more powerful than you. You will never know all of its secrets.

The Bigoted Brain

'Thug ... tart ... slob ... nerd ... airhead'

My husband's first experience of Scotland was a formative one, from which I fear he has never fully recovered. We travelled across the border to Berwick for a wedding, and booked into a not inexpensive bed and breakfast. Now the Scots do have a certain reputation for, shall we say, a propensity towards thrift. We were, however, prepared to assume that the absence of any soap in our room was an oversight – until, that is, we were sharply informed, in response to our inquiry, that the provision of soap was deemed to be the responsibility of the guest. My husband was somewhat taken aback by this. In his native New Zealand, any B&B guest upon whom large quantities of handcrafted Manuka honey soap are not lavished considers themselves very hard done by. 'So it's true, what they say about Scots', he remarked with glee, delighted to have been treated so soon to an apparent vindication of the stereotype.

But there was a far more challenging horror to greet us in the morning. We sat down to breakfast, tired and hungover after the wedding, and waited impatiently for the pot of tea to brew. Every few minutes my husband would dribble another splash of pale gold water into his cup, then return the pot to the table with an angry clatter. After about ten minutes of this, he decided that further investigation was required. He lifted the teapot lid and peered inside. His eyes, when they rose to meet mine, were wide with disbelief. In awe, he whispered to me, 'There are no tea bags in there. Not *one*!'

He was quiet and thoughtful on the long drive home. Every so often he would break the silence to ask, 'Do you suppose they use the *same* tea bag to make everyone's pot of tea?' or to speculate, 'Perhaps each table has its own dedicated bag, which is pegged up to dry on a little line, ready for the next morning.'

Possibly, given this experience, I should have been more understanding of my husband's response to my telling him about our bigoted brains. Over dinner, I explained how it is that pernicious stereotypes colour our every interpretation of others' behaviour, and even have the power to generate self-fulfilling prophecies of our stereotypical beliefs. With eloquent passion, I told him of our ignoble habit of using stereotypes to boost our egos, and the subtle but devastating effects of stereotypes on stereotyped groups. Finally, my dinner cold and untouched on my plate in noble sacrifice to his edification, I described the devious tricks the brain uses to discount evidence that contradicts our stereotypical beliefs, thus condemning us all to an eternally prejudiced and damaging perspective of our fellow humans.

'Ye-es', said my husband hesitantly, when I had finally stopped talking. 'But the Scots really *are* mean.'

As I said, given the trauma of a post-wedding breakfast without a nice strong cup of tea, I should have been more understanding. But I wasn't.

'*That*', I retorted angrily, 'is just the sort of thing an affluent white male *would* say.'

However egalitarian you may be (or think you are), your brain is stuffed with stereotypes. You may not personally subscribe to the view that women are nurturing, that black men are aggressive, or that Jews keep a tight grip on their wallets, but you can't pretend not to know that these are stereotypical traits of women, blacks and Jews. Stereotypes are a subgroup of the schemas that we met in the previous chapter ('The Secretive Brain'), the filing system the brain uses to organise information into various categories. Like all schemas, in people schemas (or stereotypes), all the information about a certain group – homosexuals, the unemployed, Asians – is closely intertwined in the brain. This means that if you use one bit of the schema – even just to be able to say 'Ah, an Asian' – then all the other parts of the Asian schema get restless. As a result, information in the Asian stereotype is more likely to be used by the brain, as it goes about the difficult job of interpreting the complicated and often ambiguous behaviour of those around us.

In a classic demonstration of this, some volunteers were subliminally primed with flashes of words (mostly negative) related to the African-American stereotype.[119] These included words such as *lazy, welfare, unemployed, ghetto* and *basketball.* Now one of the most commonly reported traits of the African-American stereotype is aggressiveness, but the researcher was careful not to include any words related to aggression in the priming. She reasoned that, it being an intimate bedfellow of the other parts of the African-American stereotype, it would get awakened by the stirrings anyway. That this indeed happened – and its effect on the volunteers' decoding of another person's behaviour – was revealed by the second part of the experiment. The volunteers were asked to give their impressions of a character called Donald. Donald did things that could be viewed as either hostile or assertive, such as refusing to pay his rent until his flat was repainted. People whose African-American stereotypes had been primed judged Donald to be significantly more hostile than did other volunteers not primed in the same way. The volunteers weren't aware that the stereotype had been activated – they hadn't even been aware of the words – but it still had the power to colour their judgment of Donald.

The disturbing implication is that when dealing with a black man, the black stereotype is primed and ready to distort his every word and deed. We might, for example, mistake the wallet he is pulling from his pocket for a gun. In 1999, four white New York police officers were acquitted of shooting an unarmed black man on the grounds that they had made this very mistake, and thought that their lives were in danger. The officers may well have been speaking the truth, but would their eyes have deceived them in the same way had their unfortunate victim, Amidou Diallo, been white? Quite possibly not, suggests research using stereotype priming.[120] Student volunteers were shown pairs of images: a face, followed by either a handgun or a hand tool. They were told to ignore the face, which flashed up briefly supposedly to signal that the next image was about to appear, and to then identify the second picture as a gun or tool as quickly as possible. Half of the time the face was black; the rest of the time it was white. The volunteers were much quicker at identifying the handguns when they were preceded by a black face, showing that perception itself was influenced by the racial priming. More disturbing still, however, was the discovery that volunteers, when under heavy pressure to classify the object quickly (as a police officer would often be), were more likely to mistake tools for handguns when they had just seen a black face. This suggests that the New York officers might have held their fire for a few extra, potentially life-saving milliseconds, had Amidou Diallo been white.

It's easy to see from these experiments – and the many others like them – how viewing other people through 'bigot goggles' helps to reinforce stereotyped beliefs. We see what we expect to see. But does it make a difference whether or not you subscribe to those beliefs in the first place? Does the genuinely open-minded liberal see others through bigot goggles just the same, or does she rise loftily above such distortions? The answer seems to depend on how the stereotype is primed. For example, a British study primed the black stereotype using only neutral words (like *Brixton, dreadlocks* and *reggae*).[121] For non-racists, this had no damaging effects on their impressions of other people's behaviour. However, even this neutral priming influenced the racists – they judged that the person they were evaluating suffered from the stereotypical faults of black people: unreliability and aggressiveness. What this suggests is that only in racists will seeing a black person automatically trigger the full-blown negative stereotype.

This is cheering, but there is an important proviso. If what is primed is the *negative* stereotype, then even the non-prejudiced are susceptible to seeing the world through the biasing lens of that stereotype. In the same British study, when pejorative priming words were used (such as *unemployed, dirty* or *crime*), even the non-racists formed a more disapproving impression of the person they had to evaluate. What this means with regard to the real world is that no-holds-barred stereotyped portrayals of people will unconsciously affect the judgments of *everyone*, not just the bigot.

What, in that case, is the effect on the decent modern man of that device most beloved of advertisers everywhere: the sexy woman (or erotic part thereof)? To find out, two groups of men were shown a tape of television adverts.[122] One group of men watched mostly sexist adverts in which women were portrayed as sex objects. The other men watched ads without any sexual imagery. Next, each volunteer was asked to do a supposedly unrelated experiment: deciding whether or not a string of letters flashed on a computer screen was a word. Men who had watched the sexist adverts, unlike the other men, were quicker to recognise sexist words like 'babe' and 'bimbo' than less offensive words like 'mother' and 'sister'. This showed that the ads had done their job of priming the 'women as sexual objects' schema.

It was then time to see how this affected the men when they had to interact with a real, live woman. The men were asked, as a favour to the experimenter, to interview a female job candidate. The influence of the sexist ads on the dynamics of this interview was extraordinary. The men who had just watched women portrayed as sex-things – even the non-sexist men – sat closer to the interviewee, flirted more, and asked her a greater number of sexually inappropriate questions, compared with the other men. The sexist adverts also biased the men's memory of the candidate, and their ability to gauge her qualifications. The sex-primed men remembered a great deal about the woman's physical appearance, but far less information that would help them to decide her suitability for the job. This didn't stop them from rating her as less competent, however. Despite this, these men were still more likely than the other group to recommend hiring the woman, perhaps because they found her more friendly and attractive than did the non-primed men. A meagre comfort, indeed, for women seeking gainful employment – especially when you consider that all of these shameful changes in the men came from them watching a few sex-pots draped over cars or around beer bottles.

This experiment doesn't just demonstrate that you should never, ever tell a woman who complains about sexist adverts to lighten up. It also highlights the second dangerous power of stereotypes: their capacity to change our *own* behaviour. In fact, you already saw this phenomenon in action in 'The Secretive Brain'. Remember, for example, the volunteers who ambled at a snail's pace down the hallway after having their 'elderly schema' primed? Benign as this may sound, the trouble begins when you add another person into the social equation. Your behaviour has a knock-on effect on their behaviour and suddenly, without anyone having an inkling about it, you have all the ingredients of a self-fulfilling prophecy. Seeing a black person triggers the stereotype of the aggressive, hostile black. You – acting in line with the stereotype – behave aggressively yourself, which in turn leads the maligned person to respond in kind. You notice their hostility and – not realising your own role in their behaviour – the stereotype is confirmed in your mind.

Vicious circles of just this sort have been seen by social psychologists. For example, white people subliminally primed with African-American faces respond in a more hostile way to a request by the experimenter to redo a tedious computer task, compared with people primed with Caucasian faces.[123] The researchers wondered whether this primed aggressiveness might, in turn, make anyone on the receiving end of it more antagonistic in return.[124] One group of volunteers had the African-American stereotype subliminally primed using faces of African-American men, whereas the control group volunteers were primed with Caucasian faces. Then the volunteers were asked to play a quiz game with another (white) person. (The volunteers' quiz partners had to be white because a black partner would also prime the African-American stereotype in the control group, and might arouse suspicions regarding the nature of the experiment.) Just as the researchers predicted, the African-American primed volunteers behaved more aggressively than volunteers primed with Caucasian faces. But what's more, this affected their quiz partner, who responded by getting bolshy right back. This didn't go unnoticed by the volunteers, who rated their partners as more hostile than did the control group volunteers.

What is most creepy about self-fulfilling stereotypes is that when you project your stereotypical beliefs onto someone, the image that gets bounced back is more a reflection of your own behaviour than of their true qualities. Yet your role in this horrible distortion goes undetected. The most well-meaning intention to be impartial when evaluating job applicants, for example, may be thoroughly undermined by your own behaviour. When white people were asked to interview a job applicant, they behaved very differently depending on whether the applicant was black or white.[125] This was despite the fact that the 'applicants' were actually stooges, carefully trained to perform in a standard manner during the interview. If the applicant was black, the interviewers kept themselves more physically distant, made more speech errors during the interview, and ended it more abruptly.

A dispiriting follow-up study showed that being

treated like a black person in this way could undermine anyone's interview performance. White Princeton University students were interviewed for a job by trained stooges. Half were given the remote, inarticulate and terse style of interview that black applicants received in the first experiment. This 'black treatment' hampered the white Princeton students: judges watching the interviews rated them as significantly less competent for the job than students given the 'white treatment'. This experiment shows that relatively subtle differences in the way that white people respond to black people, compared with whites, may undermine black job applicants' true abilities, making them seem less competent than they really are. Then, not only does *that* black person not get the job, but the impression that black people tend not to be quite up to scratch becomes engrained a little more strongly in the interviewer's mind.

Unfortunately, stereotypes don't just act on stereotyped groups *via* other people: the grubby fingerprinting can be found directly on the members of stereotyped groups. A woman in a maths class, or a black student in an exam, must both perform under the threatening shadow of the stereotype of inferiority. The anxiety that this 'stereotype threat' generates hampers their natural ability, and the stereotype is confirmed.[126] Rather surprisingly, the burden that stereotype threat brings to its bearer is remarkably easy to uncover. For instance, men sometimes outperform women at maths, particularly at very advanced levels. This has, of course, led to all sorts of claims about genetic differences in maths ability between men and women. Yet researchers interested in stereotype threat were able to magically close this gender gap (and no genetic modification required).[127] One group of university maths students were given a hard maths test. The men outperformed the women. But hold your smirks, fellas, and don't be too quick to draw conclusions. A second group of students were given exactly the same test, but were told beforehand that gender differences had never been found in how men and women scored on this particular test. When the cloud of stereotype threat was dispersed in this way, the women did every bit as well as the men. In fact, it's not only the case that stereotypes about maths are damaging to women. Men normally benefit slightly from the culturally ingrained assumption that they are naturally superior to women, an effect called 'stereotype lift'.[128] Men don't perform quite as well if you whip this booster seat away from under them by informing them that, on this occasion, their possession of certain masculine physical attributes won't help their performance.

By now, you should be developing a certain grudging awe for the number of ways in which stereotypes further themselves: the bigot goggles, the self-fulfilling prophecy, stereotype threat, and stereotype lift. Yet, you may furtively wonder, is this enough to explain why stereotypes live on, if there really is no truth to them? I will leave discussion of the 'kernel of truth' hypothesis to more courageous writers.[129] However, bear in mind that so far we have seen only the stereotype's arsenal of attack: the ways in which it distorts our judgments and behaviour. The stereotype also enjoys a strong line of defence against people inconsiderate enough to challenge our bigoted expectancies. As revealed in 'The Deluded Brain', we're rather prone to fiddling the statistics to fit our beliefs. We fall prey to illusory correlation, 'seeing' links between groups of people and traits that fit a stereotype, but don't actually exist. Are menopausal women really bad-tempered grumps, for example? According to their stereotype they are but, as one study showed, illusory correlation has much to answer for in perpetuating this moody image.[130] People hugely overestimate how often they have seen menopausal women in a stink.

Another clever way to discount people who don't fit in with your stereotyped beliefs is to pop them into a little category all of their own. As we saw in 'The Pigheaded Brain', we have a remarkable capacity to make up explanations to back up anything we happen to believe. In just the same way, we seize on handy little details to explain away the generous Jew, or the assertive woman. We will claim 'Oh, but she went to such a posh girls' school' (or 'Oh, but she went to such a rough comprehensive') to account conveniently for what seems to us to be unusual assertiveness in a woman, leaving us with no urge to update our stereotype.[131] In fact, if the person deviates enough from their stereotype, we don't even feel the need to justify ignoring the challenge that their existence presents. Their freakishness, in our eyes, is seen as grounds enough for dismissing them.[132]

This is all dispiriting enough, but there is even

more depressing news for those who do not fit the stereotypical mould of their sex. Gender 'deviants' are at risk of far worse treatment than merely being rejected as irrelevant. For instance, women who venture outside the acceptable limits set by gender stereotypes invite backlash against them. Research suggests that there are very good reasons why a woman can't 'be more like a man'. In the psychology laboratory, women who do unusually well on a 'masculine' test have been shown to have their chance of winning a prize in a quiz sabotaged by others.[133] While in a business setting, women who behave 'like men' by promoting a highly confident and competent image of themselves in an interview are judged to be less socially skilled than are men who behave just the same.[134] (Regrettably, there are also good reasons for a woman not to behave like a woman. Women who are more 'femininely' modest about their skills are seen as less competent.[135]) These backlash effects may well play an important part in encouraging women to toe the line. And so the oppressive stereotype marches on.

Stereotypes, as you will have gathered, are powerful enemies of equality. But we do have some control over their influence on our bigoted brains. We are quite capable of resisting their use. Unfortunately, however, we appear to switch our stereotypes on and off in whatever way best suits our egos. For example, if we are criticised by a woman or a black person, we use our negative stereotype of them to cast aspersions on their judgment. By disparaging them in this way, we protect our vain brains from the hurtful effects of negative feedback.[136] If, however, it is praise rather than criticism issuing forth from a female or black mouth, we miraculously manage to inhibit our negative stereotypes, and consider our evaluators to be as able as any white man at their job. As the researchers of these studies succinctly put it, 'She's fine if she praised me but incompetent if she criticized me.'

Worse still, there is evidence that we will use stereotypes to disparage anyone we can in order to make ourselves feel better, even if it was not the slandered person who made us feel bad in the first place. Researchers cast a blow to the self-esteem of half of a group of students by telling them that they had scored lower than average on an intelligence test.[137] The other students were told that they had done extremely well. Some of the ego-bruised students were then given an opportunity to jolly themselves up at someone else's expense, using a negative stereotype. All the students were asked to evaluate a job candidate. Each of them considered the very same woman, and she appeared identical in each of her interviews, in all respects but one. For some of the students she was 'Julie Goldberg', volunteer for a Jewish organisation, member of a Jewish sorority, and wearer of a Star of David necklace. To the other students she was presented as 'Maria D'Agostino', volunteer for a Catholic organisation, member of a European sorority, who bore a cross around her neck. This probably requires no further spelling out, except to say that the researchers reported that the unflattering stereotype of the 'Jewish American Princess' was well known and widely discussed on the campus at which they ran this experiment. The students were, however, good enough not to hold anything in particular against Italian women.

The researchers were most interested in the students who were still reeling from their supposed inferiority on the intelligence test, who were also given the opportunity to perform the psychological equivalent of kicking the cat, by being given a Jewish woman job applicant to evaluate. Could they be so ignoble as to deprecate this innocent woman, simply because their own noses had been put out of joint? They certainly could. Their ratings of the interviewee's personality and qualifications were far lower than everyone else's. But as cat-kickers everywhere will know, it certainly had the desired effect: their self-esteem went shooting up afterwards.

To be fair to our bigoted brains, people who want to avoid prejudiced thoughts can, and do, quash the activity of their stereotypes. However, this requires no small amount of mental effort. This means that if you are tired, distracted, or under pressure the stereotype can shake free of this restraint, returning to freedom to wreak its malignant influence.[138] When American researchers asked students to rate racist jokes using a Ha!Ha!-ometer, the students were suitably grudging with their Ha!Ha!'s.[139] Yet students who were distracted while they rated the jokes (they had to do a demanding counting and memory task at the same time) found the racist jokes much funnier. We lower our guard, too, if we feel that we have already established our egalitarian credentials.

For example, people who are given the chance to flaunt their feminist stripes by rejecting blatantly sexist statements will then sit back and rest on their laurels. These quietly complacent people are subsequently *more* likely to agree with subtly sexist statements.[140]

Indeed, research suggests that even successful attempts to stem our prejudices can backfire later. We hold the stereotype down temporarily, but it bobs right back up again with increased vigour. Researchers asked people to write a 'day in the life' story about someone in a photo, who happened to be a skinhead.[141] Some of the volunteers were asked to try to avoid stereotyping in their story. These volunteers did successfully suppress the skinhead stereotype; their stories contained far less material along the stereotypic lines of '... and then I thumped him one' and the like. However, the stereotype actually gained new strength from its brief confinement. Asked shortly afterwards to write a second passage about a skinhead, the stories of these volunteers contained far more stereotyping than the stories of the volunteers who had been left to respond naturally to their stereotypes. The rebounding of the skinhead stereotype also showed its influence when the volunteers were invited to step into a room to meet the very skinhead whose photo they had seen. The skinhead wasn't there, but his belongings were on one of the chairs. People whose skinhead stereotypes were acting with fresh force (after being damped down in the 'day in the life' task) showed their heightened disdain and fear of the skinhead by choosing to sit further away from his belongings.

Does this mean that even the Equal Opportunities lawyer, after a hard day battling for equality in the workplace, is eventually worn down by omnipotent stereotypes? Does he clutch his briefcase more closely to his side when a black man sits next to him on the bus and, once home, berate his wife for not having dinner ready on the table? The outlook, fortunately, may not be quite this bleak. People who sincerely wish to avoid stereotyping a particular group seem to be able to avoid the rebound effect that suppressing a stereotype usually brings. This motivation might be lacking in most people when it comes to skinheads, but strong enough (in at least some people) to keep less socially acceptable stereotypes about black, Asian or gay people at bay for longer. But again, we can do this only when we are mentally completely on our toes.[142]

This has been a discouraging story so far and it would be understandable if, at this point in its relating, you were to lay down the book and weep. The problem is that we need the efficiency that schemas buy us. Schemas provide a quick means of extracting and interpreting information from the complicated world around us, of forming useful generalisations, and making helpful predictions. Likewise, a bigoted brain is an efficient brain. A brain unburdened by egalitarian concerns can decide 'Thug … tart … slob … nerd … airhead', then move swiftly on to the next thing on its 'To Do' list.[143] Yet this speed comes at the cost – mostly to others – of accuracy, particularly when our schemas fail to reflect reality truthfully. We don't always have (or make available) the time, opportunity, motivation or mental resources we need to consider the rich, complex and unique personalities of everyone we encounter. Nor do we always have the time or the inclination to pause to consider whether we are in peril of being prejudiced, and attempt to compensate for it. We may not even recognise the henchmen – or women – of stereotypes when they are staring us in the face. (So ubiquitous is the image of women as sex objects, for example, that the researchers in the 'women as sex objects' priming experiment found that many of the men who watched the sexist adverts were adamant that they must have been in the control group – because the ads they saw 'weren't sexist'.)

However, social psychologists are beginning to explore what strategies might help us thwart the bigoted tendencies of our brains.[144] The fact that our unconscious will eventually help out if we consistently make the conscious effort to act in a certain way in particular types of situation – the phenomenon described in 'The Secretive Brain' – offers a glimmer of hope. For it seems that we may be able to train our brain to replace its spontaneous prejudices with more acceptable reflexes.

The first step is acknowledging your brain's unwelcome bigotry. And indeed, most of us are familiar with the disconcerting experience of a shamefully bigoted thought popping into our consciousness unbidden. You might know that you *shouldn't* feel worried about the intentions of a black man walking towards you on an empty street, yet in truth you know that you probably would. When American researchers asked a group of non-black students about the differences between their 'should' and 'would' responses to African-Americans, most admitted that they often experienced involuntary racist thoughts that were at odds with their consciously held 'colour-blind' principles.

Yet a subset of the group claimed to almost always respond to African-Americans as a good egalitarian should. You might think that they were deceiving themselves, or were perhaps trying to 'fake good' to the researchers. But in fact, they seemed to have actually managed to reprogram their bigoted brains for the better. When the researchers gave these students the joke-rating task described earlier, the students remained unamused by the racist jokes, even when they were heavily distracted while they were making their Ha!Ha! ratings. Since their brains were too busy with the attention-grabbing counting and memorising to have been able to do much work suppressing any involuntary amusement at the racist jokes, these students must have been effortlessly disdainful of humour based on black stereotypes. From interviewing people with 'would' responses to African-

Americans that remained firmly in line with their 'shoulds', the researchers were inclined to think that these exemplary individuals had managed to rid themselves of their unwanted automatic prejudices through conscious effort and rehearsal.

This, then, gives us all something to strive towards. We can be cheered by the thought that, with constant vigilance and practice, perhaps at least some of the myriad situations that invite stereotyping might automatically come to trigger our defences against prejudice. However, it is likely to be a longer and more arduous walk to freedom from bigotry than many of us are able to withstand.

Particularly in a Scottish bed and breakfast without a nice strong cup of tea to fortify us.

Epilogue

So what are we to make of ourselves now? Through the course of this book, we've seen that the brain that we trust so implicitly to do the right thing by us has a mind of its own. An adroit manipulator of information, it leaves us staring at a mere façade of reality. Vanity shields us from unpalatable truths about ourselves. Irrationality clouds our judgment, leaving us vulnerable to errors and delusions – a situation only worsened by our pigheadedness. The emotions add a gloss of their own, colouring and confusing our opinions, while unobtrusively masterminding our behaviour and sense of being. The secretive unconscious also delights in a handful of strings to pull, concealing from us many of the true influences on our thoughts and deeds. And, careless of our good intentions, the brain's ignoble use of stereotypes blurs our view of others to an all but inevitable bigotry.

Being confronted with the evidence of these slick and resourceful window-dressings of the brain is unsettling, and rightly so. A brain with a mind of its own belies our strong sense that the world is just as it seems to us, and our misguided belief that our vision of 'out there' is sharp and true. Even more troubling, perhaps, is to learn of the farce that passes for self-knowledge. Our conception of ourselves, we have learned, is ever-changing, fluidly adapting itself to our circumstances and moods, and the petulant demands of self-esteem. True motives, too, remain disturbingly obscure much of the time, when the devious brain hides from us the real sources of our actions and views.

However, while the veil our brain stealthily drapes over reality can never be whipped away entirely, we should not be completely disheartened. Knowledge of the many common machinations of the brain does at least provide modest scope to guard against them. Mental events that manipulate our brains – emotions, moods, schemas and stereotypes, for example – can lose some of their effect when we are aware of their potential to influence us. Recall the experiment described in 'The Emotional Brain', in which volunteers were asked about their life satisfaction on rainy or sunny days. Volunteers asked about the weather beforehand were less affected by weather-induced mood when giving their ratings than were volunteers not alerted to the current climatic conditions. Of course, the notorious British propensity for using the weather as an opening conversational gambit should offer protection against this particular influence on our thoughts. But still, remaining mindful of our susceptibility to other sources of prejudicing emotional fallout – a bad day at work, a coffee on the house, some bloody psychologist ringing up uninvited and wittering on about the weather – can only help compensate against it.

It's also encouraging that determined efforts on our part to see the world accurately can help counteract distortion. If precision is important enough to us, we are capable of greater conscientiousness in gathering and considering our evidence. If it is important enough to you not to stereotype a particular group, for example, then with a little effort you will succeed, as described in 'The Bigoted Brain'. Nor, fortunately, must we be completely reliant on people motivating themselves to remove their bigot goggles. Making people accountable for their judgments of others goes a long way towards focusing their vision of other people with greater clarity.[145]

Best of all, we can recruit the brain's freelance mind to use to our own advantage – as when we consciously train the 'mental butler' of our unconscious mental life efficiently and effortlessly to fulfil our aspirations. With some exertion on our part, the unconscious can come to automatically respond to certain situations in a manner that is in line with our conscious wishes. Vigilant weight-watchers, described in 'The Secretive Brain', trained their mental butlers to respond to calorific temptations with an instant pursing of the lips and a shake of the head. Similarly, it seems possible for us to cajole our brain into replacing its unwanted illiberal reactions to stereotyped groups with more enlightened attitudes.

Yet with this faint hope – that we are not entirely defenceless martyrs to the fictions of the brain – comes responsibility. We owe a duty to ourselves, and to others, to lessen the harmful effects of the brain's various shams, whenever we can. To be all eyes and ears for influences that may lead us astray when we are making important decisions. To be more tolerant of opposing viewpoints, however much it may seem that we are on the side of the angels. To resist the easy complicity of stereotypes when judging others. To endeavour to put in the necessary groundwork to bring the unruly actions of the unconscious in line with our principles and values. And not to exploit the loose leash of other people's brains in order to sell more soft drinks.

Above all, we should try to remain alert always to the distortions and deceptions of our wayward brains. For they are always with us.

Notes and References

THE VAIN BRAIN

1 J.M. Nuttin (1985), 'Narcissism beyond Gestalt and awareness: the name-letter effect', *European Journal of Social Psychology*, 15: 353–61.

2 For example, N. Epley and D. Dunning (2000), 'Feeling "holier than thou": are self-serving assessments produced by errors in self- or social prediction?' *Journal of Personality and Social Psychology*, 79: 861–75; C. Heath (1999), 'On the social psychology of agency relationships: lay theories of motivation overemphasize extrinsic incentives', *Organizational Behavior and Human Decision Processes*, 78: 25–62; O. Svenson (1981), 'Are we all less risky and more skillful than our fellow drivers?' *Acta Psychologica*, 47: 143–8.

3 D. Dunning, J.A. Meyerowitz and A.D. Holzberg (2002), 'Ambiguity and self-evaluation: the role of idiosyncratic trait definition in self-serving assess-

ments of ability', in T. Gilovich *et al.* (eds), *Heuristics and Biases: The Psychology of Intuitive Judgment*, New York, NY: Cambridge University Press (pp. 324–33).

4   D. Dunning, M. Perie and A. L. Story (1991), 'Self-serving prototypes of social categories', *Journal of Personality and Social Psychology*, 16: 957–68.

5   J. D. Campbell (1986), 'Similarity and uniqueness: the effects of attribute type, relevance, and individual differences in self-esteem and depression', *Journal of Personality and Social Psychology*, 50: 281–94.

6   For example, J. R. Larson (1977), 'Evidence for a self-serving bias in the attribution of causality', *Journal of Personality*, 45: 430–41.

7   W. K. Campbell and C. Sedikides (1999), 'Self-threat magnifies the self-serving bias: a meta-analytic integration', *Review of General Psychology*, 3: 23–43.

8   E. Pronin, D. Y. Lin and L. Ross (2002), 'The bias blind spot: perceptions of bias in self versus others', *Personality and Social Psychology Bulletin*, 28: 369–81.

9   L. J. Sanna and E. C. Chang (2003), 'The past is not what it used to be: optimists' use of retroactive pessimism to diminish the sting of failure', *Journal of Research in Personality*, 37: 388–404.

10 T. W. Smith, C. R. Snyder and M. M. Handelsman (1982), 'On the self-serving function of an academic wooden leg: test anxiety as a self-handicapping strategy', *Journal of Personality and Social Psychology*, 42: 314–21.

11 J.M. Burger and R.M. Huntzinger (1985), 'Temporal effects on attributions for one's own behavior: the role of task outcome', *Journal of Experimental Social Psychology*, 21: 247–61.

12 C. Sedikides and J.D. Green (2000), 'On the self-protective nature of inconsistency-negativity management: using the person memory paradigm to examine self-referent memory', *Journal of Personality and Social Psychology*, 79: 906–22.

13 H. Markus and E. Wurf (1987), The dynamic self-concept: a social psychological perspective', *Annual Review of Psychology*, 38: 299–337.

14 Z. Kunda and R. Sanitioso (1989), 'Motivated changes in the self-concept', *Journal of Experimental Social Psychology*, 25: 272–85.

15 R. Sanitioso, Z. Kunda and G.T. Fong (1990), 'Motivated recruitment of autobiographical memories', *Journal of Personality and Social Psychology*, 59: 229–41.

16 R. Sanitioso and R. Wlordarski (2004), 'In search of information that confirms a desired self-perception: motivated processing of social feedback and choice of social interactions', *Personality and Social Psychology Bulletin*, 30: 412–22.

17 Z. Kunda (1987), 'Motivated inference: self-serving generation and evaluation of causal theories', *Journal of Personality and Social Psychology*, 53: 636–47.

18 R.S. Wyer and D. Frey (1983), 'The effects of feedback about self and others on the recall and judgments of

feedback-relevant information', *Journal of Experimental Social Psychology*, 19: 540–59.

19 For summary, see Z. Kunda (1990), 'The case for motivated reasoning', *Psychological Bulletin*, 108: 480–98.

20 R. Sanitioso and R. Wlordarski (2004), 'In search of information that confirms a desired self-perception: motivated processing of social feedback and choice of social interactions', *Personality and Social Psychology Bulletin*, 30: 412–22.

21 A. M. Rosenthal (1999), *Thirty-eight Witnesses: The Kitty Genovese Case*, Berkeley, CA: University of California Press.

22 See C. R. Snyder (1985), 'Collaborative companions: the relationship of self-deception and excuse making', in M. W. Martin (ed.), *Self-deception and Self-understanding: New Essays in Philosophy and Psychology*, Lawrence, KS: University of Kansas Press (pp. 35–51).

23 See M. J. Lerner (1980), *The Belief in a Just World: A Fundamental Delusion*, New York: Plenum Press.

24 Z. Kunda (1987), 'Motivated inference: self-serving generation and evaluation of causal theories', *Journal of Personality and Social Psychology*, 53: 636–47.

25 C. R. Snyder (1978), 'The "illusion" of uniqueness', *Journal of Humanistic Psychology*, 18: 33–41.

26 Z. Kunda (1987), 'Motivated inference: self-serving generation and evaluation of causal theories', *Journal of Personality and Social Psychology*, 53: 636–47.

27 P.H. Ditto and D.F. Lopez (1992), 'Motivated skepticism: use of differential decision criteria for preferred and nonpreferred conclusions', *Journal of Personality and Social Psychology*, 63: 568–84.

28 G.A. Quattrone and A. Tversky (1984), 'Causal versus diagnostic contingencies: on self-deception and on the voter's illusion', *Journal of Personality and Social Psychology*, 46: 237–48.

29 See S.E. Taylor and J.D. Brown (1988), 'Illusion and well-being: a social psychological perspective on mental health', *Psychological Bulletin*, 103: 193–210.

30 See R.J. Trotter (1987), 'Stop blaming yourself', *Psychology Today*, 21: 31–9.

31 See C.R. Snyder and R.L. Higgins (1988), 'Excuses: their effective role in the negotiation of reality', *Psychological Bulletin*, 104: 23–35.

32 See S.E. Taylor and J.D. Brown (1988), 'Illusion and well-being: a social psychological perspective on mental health', *Psychological Bulletin*, 103: 193–210.

33 T. Pyszczynski, J. Greenberg, S. Solomon, J. Arndt and J. Schimel (2004), 'Why do people need self-esteem? A theoretical and empirical review', *Psychological Bulletin*, 130: 435–68.

THE EMOTIONAL BRAIN

34 A. Bechara, H. Damasio and A.R. Damasio (2000), 'Emotion, decision making and the orbitofrontal cortex', *Cerebral Cortex*, 10: 295–307.

35 P.J. Eslinger and A.R. Damasio (1985), 'Severe distur-
    bance of higher cognition after bilateral frontal lobe
    ablation: Patient EVR', *Neurology*, 35: 1731–41.

36 J.L. Saver and A.R. Damasio (1991), 'Preserved access
    and processing of social knowledge in a patient with
    acquired sociopathy due to ventromedial frontal
    damage', *Neuropsychologia*, 29: 1241–9.

37 A.R. Damasio, D. Tranel and H. Damasio (1990),
    'Individuals with sociopathic behavior caused by
    frontal damage fail to respond autonomically to
    social stimuli', *Behavioral Brain Research*, 41: 81–94.

38 A. Bechara, H. Damasio and A.R. Damasio (2000),
    'Emotion, decision making and the orbitofrontal
    cortex', *Cerebral Cortex*, 10: 295–307.

39 J. Haidt (2001), 'The emotional dog and its rational
    tail: a social intuitionist approach to moral judgment',
    Psychological Review, 108: 814–34.

40 J. Haidt and M.A. Hersh (2001), 'Sexual morality:
    the cultures and emotions of conservatives and liberals',
    Journal of Applied Social Psychology, 31: 191–221.

41 Discussed in R.F. Baumeister and L.S. Newman
    (1994), 'Self-regulation of cognitive inference and
    decision processes', *Personality and Social Psychology
    Bulletin*, 20: 3–19.

42 For discussion of the role of arousal in emotion, see
    G. Mandler (1984), *Mind and Emotion: Psychology of
    Emotion and Stress*, New York: W.W. Norton.

43 A.F. Ax (1953), 'The physiological differentiation

between fear and anger in humans', *Psychosomatic Medicine*, 15: 433–42.

44 According to G. Mandler (1984), *Mind and Emotion: Psychology of Emotion and Stress*, New York: W.W. Norton.

45 J.R. Cantor, D. Zillman and J. Bryant (1975), 'Enhancement of experienced sexual arousal in response to erotic stimuli through misattribution of unrelated residual excitation', *Journal of Personality and Social Psychology*, 32: 69–75.

46 N. Schwartz, F. Strack, D. Kommer and D. Wagner (1987), 'Soccer, rooms, and the quality of your life: mood effects on judgments of satisfaction with life in general and with specific domains', *European Journal of Social Psychology*, 17: 69–79; E.J. Johnson and A. Tversky (1983), 'Affect, generalization, and the perception of risk', *Journal of Personality and Social Psychology*, 45: 20–31; L.M. Isbell and R.S. Wyer (1999), 'Correcting for mood-induced bias in the evaluation of political candidates: the role of intrinsic and extrinsic motivation', *Personality and Social Psychology Bulletin*, 25: 237–49.

47 A.M. Isen, T.E. Shalker, M. Clark and L. Karp (1978), 'Affect, accessibility of material in memory, and behavior: a cognitive loop?' *Journal of Personality and Social Psychology*, 36: 1–12.

48 P. Salovey and D. Birnbaum (1989), 'Influence of mood on health-relevant cognitions', *Journal of*

Personality and Social Psychology, 57: 539–51; J.P. Forgas (1994), 'Sad and guilty? Affective influences on the explanation of conflict in close relationships', *Journal of Personality and Social Psychology*, 66: 56–68; V.M. Esses and M.P. Zanna (1995), 'Mood and the expression of ethnic stereotypes', *Journal of Personality and Social Psychology*, 69: 1052–68.

49 See, for example, J.P. Forgas (1995), 'Mood and judgment: the Affect Infusion Model (AIM)', *Psychological Bulletin*, 117: 39–66.

50 N. Schwartz and G.L. Clore (1983), 'Mood, misattribution, and judgments of well-being: informative and directive functions of affective states', *Journal of Personality and Social Psychology*, 45: 513–23.

51 See C. Senior, E. Hunter, M.V. Lambert *et al.* (2001), 'Depersonalisation', *The Psychologist*, 14: 128–32.

52 M. Sierra, C. Senior, J. Dalton *et al.* (2002), 'Autonomic response in depersonalization disorder', *Archives of General Psychiatry*, 59: 833–8.

53 M.L. Phillips, N. Medford, C. Senior *et al.* (2001), 'Depersonalization disorder: thinking without feeling', *Psychiatry Research: Neuroimaging Section*, 108: 145–60.

54 For reports of experiences of depersonalisation patients see, for example, S. Bockner (1949), 'The depersonalization syndrome: report of a case', *Journal of Mental Science*, 93: 968–71; G. Simeon, S. Gross, O. Guralnik *et al.* (1997), 'Feeling unreal: 30 cases of

DSM-III-R Depersonalization Disorder', *American Journal of Psychiatry*, 154: 1107–13.

55 A suggestion made by A.R. Damasio (1996), *Descartes' Error*, London: Macmillan.

56 See A.W. Young and K. Leafhead (1996), 'Betwixt life and death: case studies of the Cotard delusion', in P.W. Halligan and J.C. Marshall (eds), *Method in Madness: Case Studies in Cognitive Neuropsychiatry*, Hove, East Sussex: Erlbaum (UK) Taylor and Francis (pp. 147–71).

The Deluded Brain

57 The current diagnostic definition of delusion, according to the *Diagnostic and Statistical Manual IV*, is: 'a false belief based on incorrect inference about external reality that is firmly sustained despite what almost everyone else believes and despite what constitutes incontrovertible and obvious proof or evidence to the contrary' (American Psychiatric Association, 1994: p. 765). For discussion of difficulties in adequately defining delusions, see B.V. Halligan and H. Ellis (2003), 'Beliefs about delusions', *The Psychologist*, 16: 418–23.

58 See B.A. Maher (1999), 'Anomalous experience in everyday life: its significance for psychopathology', *The Monist*, 82: 547–70. Also E. Cardeña, S.J. Lynn and S. Krippner (eds) (2000), *Varieties of Anomalous Experience: Examining the Scientific Evidence*,

Washington, DC: American Psychological Association.

59 Z. Kunda, G.T. Fong, R. Sanitioso and E. Reber (1993), 'Directional questions direct self-conceptions', *Journal of Experimental Social Psychology*, 29: 63–86.

60 E. Shafir (1983), 'Choosing versus rejecting: why some options are both better and worse than others', *Memory and Cognition*, 21: 546–56.

61 L.J. Chapman and J.P. Chapman (1969), 'Illusory correlation as an obstacle to the use of valid diagnostic signs', *Journal of Abnormal Psychology*, 74: 271–80.

62 For illuminating discussion on the power of expectations with regard to the 'Premenstrual Syndrome', see C. Tavris (1992), *The Mismeasure of Women: Why Women Are Not the Better Sex, the Inferior Sex, or the Opposite Sex*, New York: Touchstone.

63 See H.D. Ellis and M.B. Lewis (2001), 'Capgras delusion: a window on face recognition', *Trends in Cognitive Sciences*, 5: 149–56.

64 D.N. Anderson and E. Williams (1994), 'The delusion of inanimate doubles', *Psychopathology*, 27: 220–5.

65 H.D. Ellis, A.W. Young, A.H. Quayle and K.W. De Pauw (1997), 'Reduced autonomic responses to faces in Capgras delusion', *Proceedings of the Royal Society of London Series B, Biological Sciences*, 264 (1384): 1085–92.

66 H.D. Ellis and A.W. Young (1990), 'Accounting for delusional misidentifications', *British Journal of Psychiatry*, 157: 239–48.

67 For example, M.P. Alexander, D.T. Stuss and D.F. Benson (1979), 'Capgras syndrome: a reduplicative phenomenon', *Neurology*, 28: 334–9.

68 See P.A. Garety and D.R. Hemsley (1994), *Delusions: Investigations in the Psychology of Delusional Reasoning*, Hove, East Sussex: Psychology Press.

69 P.A. Garety, D.R. Hemsley and S. Wessely (1991), 'Reasoning in deluded schizophrenic and paranoid patients: biases in performance on a probabilistic inference task', *Journal of Nervous and Mental Disease*, 179: 194–201.

70 For criticisms of the 'jumping to conclusions' hypothesis, see B.A. Maher and M. Spitzer (1993), 'Delusions', in P.B. Sutker and H.E. Adams (eds), *Comprehensive Handbook of Psychopathology*, 2nd edn, New York: Plenum Press (pp. 263–93).

71 P.C. Wason and P.N. Johnson-Laird (1972), *Psychology of Reasoning: Structure and Content*, London: Batsford (pp. 229–39).

72 For example, R. Kemp, S. Chua, P. McKenna and A. David (1997), 'Reasoning and delusions', *British Journal of Psychiatry*, 170: 398–405; R.P. Bentall and H.F. Young (1996), 'Sensible hypothesis testing in deluded, depressed and normal subjects', *British Journal of Psychiatry*, 168: 372–5.

73 These are the 'two-factor' models; for example, M. Davies, M. Coltheart, R. Langdon and N. Breen (2001), 'Monothematic delusions: towards a two-

factor account', *Philosophy, Psychiatry and Psychology*, 8: 133–58.

74 B.A. Maher (1999), 'Anomalous experience in everyday life: its significance for psychopathology', *The Monist*, 82: 547–70.

75 C.D. Frith (1992), *The Cognitive Neuropsychology of Schizophrenia*, Hove: LEA.

76 Reported in B.A. Maher (1988), 'Anomalous experience and delusional thinking: the logic of explanations', in T.F. Oltmanns and B.A. Maher (eds), *Delusional Beliefs*, New York: John Wiley and Sons.

77 E.R. Peters, S.A. Joseph and P.A. Garety (1999), 'Measurement of delusional ideation in the normal population: introducing the PDI (Peters *et al.* Delusions Inventory)', *Schizophrenia Bulletin*, 25: 553–76.

78 *Time*/CNN (15 June 1997), *Poll: U.S. hiding knowledge of aliens* [CNN interactive poll posted on the internet], retrieved on 22 November 2004 from: http://www.cnn.com/US/9706/15/ufo.poll/index.html

79 E.R. Peters, S.A. Joseph and P.A. Garety (1999), 'Measurement of delusional ideation in the normal population: introducing the PDI (Peters *et al.* Delusions Inventory)', *Schizophrenia Bulletin*, 25: 553–76.

80 This is the view espoused by Brendan Maher.

81 For example, non-psychiatric patients who experience hallucinations are more likely to be married, to

be happy to talk about their voices, and to have positive voice experiences, than psychiatric hallucinators. There don't appear to be great differences in the hallucinatory experiences *per se*. See R.P. Bentall (2000), 'Hallucinatory experiences', in E. Cardeña, S.J. Lynn and S. Krippner (eds), *Varieties of Anomalous Experience: Examining the Scientific Evidence*, Washington DC: American Psychological Association (pp. 85–120).

THE PIGHEADED BRAIN

82 D. Sedaris (2004), *Dress Your Family in Corduroy and Denim*, London: Abacus (pp. 129–30).

83 T.R. Caretta and R.L. Moreland (1982), 'Nixon and Watergate: a field demonstration of belief perseverance', *Personality and Social Psychology Bulletin*, 8: 446–53.

84 A.J. Stewart, J.G. Webb, D. Giles and D. Hewitt (1956), 'Preliminary communication: malignant disease in childhood and diagnostic irradiation in utero', *Lancet*, 447. For details of Alice Stewart's research, see G. Greene (1999), *The Woman Who Knew Too Much: Alice Stewart and the Secrets of Radiation*, Ann Arbor: University of Michigan Press.

85 The classic demonstration of this is C.G. Lord, L. Ross and M.R. Lepper (1979), 'Biased assimilation and attitude polarization: the effects of prior theories on subsequently considered evidence', *Journal of*

Personality and Social Psychology, 37: 2098–109. See also G.D. Munro and P.H. Ditto (1997), 'Biased assimilation, attitude polarization, and affect in reactions to stereotype-relevant scientific information', *Personality and Social Psychology Bulletin*, 23: 636–53; K. Edwards and E.E. Smith (1996), 'A disconfirmation bias in the evaluation of arguments', *Journal of Personality and Social Psychology*, 71: 5–24.

86 K. Edwards and E.E. Smith (1996), 'A disconfirmation bias in the evaluation of arguments', *Journal of Personality and Social Psychology*, 71: 5–24.

87 M.J. Mahoney (1977), 'Publication prejudices: an experimental study of confirmatory bias in the peer review system', *Cognitive Therapy and Research*, 1: 161–75.

88 G. Greene (1999), *The Woman Who Knew Too Much: Alice Stewart and the Secrets of Radiation*, Ann Arbor: University of Michigan Press.

89 See, for example, R. Rosenthal (2002), 'Experimenter and clinician effects in scientific inquiry and clinical practice', *Prevention and Treatment*, 5; R. Rosenthal (1994), 'Interpersonal expectancy effects: a 30-year perspective', *Current Directions in Psychological Science*, 3: 176–9.

90 R. Rosenthal and L. Jacobson (1968), *Pygmalion in the Classroom: Teacher Expectation and Pupils' Intellectual Development*, New York: Holt, Rinehart and Winston, Inc.

91 R.P. Abelson (1986), 'Beliefs are like possessions',

Journal for the Theory of Social Behaviour, 16: 223–50.

92 L. Ross, M.R. Lepper and M. Hubbard (1975), 'Perseverance in self-perception and social perception: biased attributional processes in the debriefing paradigm', *Journal of Personality and Social Psychology*, 32: 880–92.

93 M.R. Lepper, L. Ross and R.R. Lau (1986), 'Persistence of inaccurate beliefs about the self: perseverance effects in the classroom', *Journal of Personality and Social Psychology*, 50: 482–91.

94 L. Ross, M.R. Lepper, F. Stack and J. Steinmetz (1977), 'Social explanation and social expectation: effects of real and hypothetical explanations on subjective likelihood', *Journal of Personality and Social Psychology*, 35: 817–29.

95 J. Fleming and A.J. Arrowood (1979), 'Information processing and the perseverance of discredited self-perceptions', *Personality and Social Psychology Bulletin*, 5: 201–5.

96 R.E. Petty and J.T. Cacioppo (1986), 'The elaboration likelihood model of persuasion', in L. Berkowitz (ed.), *Advances in Experimental Social Psychology*, vol. 19, Orlando, FL: Academic Press (pp. 123–205).

97 D.T. Gilbert, R.W. Tafarodi and P.S. Malone (1993), 'You can't not believe everything you read', *Journal of Personality and Social Psychology*, 65: 221–33. See also D.T. Gilbert (1991), 'How mental systems believe', *American Psychologist*, 46: 107–19.

98 D.M. Wegner, R. Wenzlaff, R.M. Kerker and A.E. Beattie (1981), 'Incrimination through innuendo: can media questions become public answers?' *Journal of Personality and Social Psychology*, 40: 822–32.

99 J.D. Lieberman and J.D. Arndt (2000), 'Understanding the limits of limiting instructions: social psychological explanations for the failures of instructions to disregard pretrial publicity and other inadmissible evidence', *Psychology, Public Policy and Law*, 6: 677–711.

100 Richard Cohen, *Washington Post*, February 1991.

THE SECRETIVE BRAIN

101 J.A. Bargh and T.L. Chartrand (1999), 'The unbearable automaticity of being', *American Psychologist*, 54: 462–79.

102 R.F. Baumeister, E. Bratslavsky, M. Muraven and D.M. Tice (1998), 'Ego depletion: is the active self a limited resource?' *Journal of Personality and Social Psychology*, 74: 1252–65.

103 See J.A. Bargh and K. Barndollar (1996), 'Automaticity in action: the unconscious as repository of chronic goals and motives', in P.M. Gollwitzer and J.A. Bargh (eds), *The Psychology of Action: Linking Cognition and Motivation to Behavior*, New York: The Guilford Press.

104 G.M. Fitzsimons and J.A. Bargh (2003), 'Thinking of you: nonconscious pursuit of interpersonal goals

associated with relationship partners', *Journal of Personality and Social Psychology*, 84: 148–64.

105 D.T. Gilbert and J.G. Hixon (1991), 'The trouble of thinking: activation and application of stereotypes', *Journal of Personality and Social Psychology*, 68: 509–17.

106 J. Shah (2003), 'Automatic for the people: how representations of significant others implicitly affect goal pursuit', *Journal of Personality and Social Psychology*, 84: 661–81.

107 G.M. Fitzsimons and J.A. Bargh (2003), 'Thinking of you: nonconscious pursuit of interpersonal goals associated with relationship partners', *Journal of Personality and Social Psychology*, 84: 148–64.

108 J.A. Bargh, M. Chen and L. Burrows (1996), 'Automaticity of social behavior: direct effects of trait construct and stereotype activation on action', *Journal of Personality and Social Psychology*, 71: 230–44.

109 A. Dijksterhuis and A. van Knippenberg (1998), 'The relation between perception and behavior, or how to win a game of Trivial Pursuit', *Journal of Personality and Social Psychology*, 74: 865–77.

110 J.A. Bargh, M. Chen and L. Burrows (1996), 'Automaticity of social behavior: direct effects of trait construct and stereotype activation on action', *Journal of Personality and Social Psychology*, 71: 230–44.

111 T.E. Moore (1982), 'Subliminal advertising: what you see is what you get', *Journal of Marketing*, 46: 38–47.

112 For discussion of the role of priming in consumer research, see J.A. Bargh (2002), 'Losing consciousness: automatic influences on consumer judgment, behavior, and motivation', *Journal of Consumer Research*, 29: 280–5.

113 K.C. Berridge and P. Winkielman (2003), 'What is an unconscious emotion? (The case for unconscious "liking")', *Cognition and Emotion*, 17: 181–211.

114 E.J. Strahan, S.J. Spencer and M.P. Zanna (2002), 'Subliminal priming and persuasion: striking while the iron is hot', *Journal of Experimental Social Psychology*, 38: 556–68.

115 A. Fischbach, R.S. Friedman and A.W. Kruglanski (2003), 'Leading us not into temptation: momentary allurements elicit overriding goal activation', *Journal of Personality and Social Psychology*, 84: 296–309.

116 A.G. Greenwald, E.R. Spangenberg, A.R. Pratkanis and J. Eskenazi (1991), 'Double-blind tests of subliminal self-help audiotapes', *Psychological Science*, 2: 119–22.

117 D.M. Wegner (2002), *The Illusion of Conscious Will*, Cambridge, MA: MIT Press. See also D.M. Wegner (2003), 'The mind's best trick: how we experience conscious will', *Trends in Cognitive Sciences*, 7: 65–9.

118 B. Libet, C.A. Gleason, E.W. Wright and D.K. Pearl (1983), 'Time of conscious intention to act in relation to onset of cerebral activities (readiness-potential): the unconscious initiation of a freely voluntary act',

Brain, 106: 623–42. For further discussion of this study, see B. Libet (1985), 'Unconscious cerebral initiative and the role of conscious will in voluntary action', *Behavioral and Brain Sciences*, 8: 529–66.

THE BIGOTED BRAIN

119 P. Devine (1989), 'Stereotypes and prejudice: their automatic and controlled components', *Journal of Personality and Social Psychology*, 56: 5–18.

120 K. B. Payne (2001), 'Prejudice and perception: the role of automatic and controlled processes in misperceiving a weapon', *Journal of Personality and Social Psychology*, 81: 181–92.

121 L. Lepore and R. Brown (1997), 'Category and stereotype activation: is prejudice inevitable?' *Journal of Personality and Social Psychology*, 72: 275–87.

122 L. A. Rudman and E. Borgida (1995), 'The afterglow of construct accessibility: the behavioral consequences of priming men to view women as sexual objects', *Journal of Experimental Social Psychology*, 31: 493–517.

123 J. A. Bargh, M. Chen and L. Burrows (1996), 'Automaticity of social behavior: direct effects of trait construct and stereotype activation on action', *Journal of Personality and Social Psychology*, 71: 230–44.

124 M. Chen and J. A. Bargh (1997), 'Nonconscious behavioral confirmation processes: the self-fulfilling consequences of automatic stereotype activation',

Journal of Experimental Social Psychology, 33: 541–60.

125 C.O. Word, M.P. Zanna and J. Cooper (1974), 'The nonverbal mediation of self-fulfilling prophecies in interracial interaction', *Journal of Experimental Social Psychology*, 10: 109–20.

126 See C.M. Steele (1997), 'A threat in the air: how stereotypes shape intellectual identity and performance', *American Psychologist*, 52: 613–29.

127 S.J. Spencer, C.M. Steele and D.M. Quin (1999), 'Stereotype threat and women's math performance', *Journal of Experimental Social Psychology*, 35: 4–28.

128 G.M. Walton and G.L. Cohen (2003), 'Stereotype lift', *Journal of Experimental Social Psychology*, 39: 456–67.

129 See L. Jussim (1991), 'Social perception and social reality: a reflection-construction model', *Psychological Review*, 98: 54–73.

130 A. Marcus-Newhall, S. Thompson and C. Thomas (2001), 'Examining a gender stereotype: menopausal women', *Journal of Applied Social Psychology*, 31: 695–719.

131 Z. Kunda and K.C. Oleson (1995), 'Maintaining stereotypes in the face of disconfirmation: constructing grounds for subtyping deviants', *Journal of Personality and Social Psychology*, 68: 565–79.

132 Z. Kunda and K.C. Oleson (1997), 'When exceptions prove the rule: how extremity of deviance determines the impact of deviant examples on stereotypes', *Journal of Personality and Social Psychology*, 72: 965–79.

133 L.A. Rudman and K. Fairchild (2004), 'Reactions to counterstereotypic behavior: the role of backlash in cultural stereotype maintenance', *Journal of Personality and Social Psychology*, 87: 157–76.

134 L.A. Rudman and P. Glick (1999), 'Feminized management and backlash toward agentic women: the hidden costs to women of a kinder, gentler image of middle managers', *Journal of Personality and Social Psychology*, 77: 743–62.

135 L.A. Rudman (1998), 'Self-promotion as a risk factor for women: the costs and benefits of counterstereotypical impression management', *Journal of Personality and Social Psychology*, 74: 629–45.

136 L. Sinclair and Z. Kunda (1999), 'Reactions to a black professional: motivated inhibition and activation of conflicting stereotypes', *Journal of Personality and Social Psychology*, 77: 885–904; L. Sinclair and Z. Kunda (2000), 'Motivated stereotyping of women: she's fine if she praised me but incompetent if she criticized me', *Personality and Social Psychology Bulletin*, 26: 1329–42.

137 S. Fein and S.J. Spencer (1997), 'Prejudice as self-image maintenance: affirming the self through derogating others', *Journal of Personality and Social Psychology*, 73: 31–44.

138 See Z. Kunda and S.J. Spencer (2003), 'When do stereotypes come to mind and when do they color judgment? A goal-based theoretical framework for

stereotype activation and application', *Psychological Bulletin*, 129: 522–44.

139 M.J. Monteith and C.I. Voils (1998), 'Proneness to prejudiced responses: toward understanding the authenticity of self-reported discrepancies', *Journal of Personality and Social Psychology*, 75: 901–16.

140 B. Monin and D.T. Miller (2001), 'Moral credentials and the expression of prejudice', *Journal of Personality and Social Psychology*, 81: 5–16.

141 C.N. Macrae, G.V. Bodenhausen, A.B. Milne and J. Jetten (1994), 'Out of mind but back in sight: stereotypes on the rebound', *Journal of Personality and Social Psychology*, 67: 808–17.

142 See M.J. Monteith, J.W. Sherman and P. Devine (1998), 'Suppression as a stereotype control strategy', *Personality and Social Psychology Review*, 2: 63–82.

143 C.N. Macrae, A.B. Milne and G.V. Bodenhausen (1994), 'Stereotypes as energy-saving devices: a peek inside the cognitive toolbox', *Journal of Personality and Social Psychology*, 66: 37–47.

144 See M.J. Monteith (1993), 'Self-regulation of prejudiced responses: implications for progress in prejudice-reduction efforts', *Journal of Personality and Social Psychology*, 65: 469–85; M.J. Monteith, L. Ashburn-Nardo, C.I. Voils and A.M. Czopp (2002), 'Putting the brakes on prejudice: on the development and operation of cues for control', *Journal of Personality and Social Psychology*, 83: 1029–50.

EPILOGUE

145 E. P. Thompson, G. B. Moskowitz, S. Chaiken and J. A. Bargh (1994), 'Accuracy motivation attenuates covert priming: the systematic reprocessing of social information', *Journal of Personality and Social Psychology*, 66: 474–89.

Index